BY JUNCTION

GCR

LMS
N° 10127

& Y Rᵞ Cᵒ
ORWICH

CALEDONIAN
37255
RAILWAY

C.W.
17774

3669

8

E EASTWOOD
BUILDER
CHESTERFIELD

TON ROAD

BICCLESWADE

MR

LANCASHIRE & YORKSHIRE Rᵞ Cᵒ

I M
STANDARD
12 TONS
40346

C.W.R
STANDARD
12 TONS
33937

STRATFORD UPON AVON & MIDLAND
JUNCTION RAILWAY
BEWARE OF TRAINS.
TRESPASSERS WILL BE PROSECUTED
By Order.

GREAT NORTHERN
— RAILWAY —
BEWARE OF THE TRAINS
LOOK BOTH UP AND DOWN
THE LINE
BEFORE YOU CROSS

MIDLAND & EASTERN RAILWAY

"MIDLAND" RAILWAY.

R.
SENERS
LINE

D1389503

(1975)

£5

1816.

Railway Relics and Regalia

General Editor
P. B. WHITEHOUSE

Country Life

Published for Country Life by
The Hamlyn Publishing Group Limited
London · New York · Sydney · Toronto
Astronaut House, Feltham, Middlesex, England
Originated, designed and produced by
Trewin Copplestone Publishing Ltd, London
© Trewin Copplestone Publishing Ltd 1975
Filmsetting and origination
by Photoprint Plates Ltd,
Rayleigh, Essex
Printed in Great Britain by
Chapel River Press, Andover, Hants

ISBN 0 600 37572 2

Contents

Acknowledgement

The Editor and the Publisher would like to thank not only those experts who have provided chapters and other advice in the making of this book but also the many others who have generously given of their knowledge and skill. Among them are: John Adams, G. S. Cattell, M. V. E. Dunn, J. Edgington, Ann Hill, B. Hinchley, W. Kirby, G. Lund, J. H. Price, E. S. Russell, C. M. Whitehouse

Abbreviations

Names of railway companies are abbreviated as follows:

B&NCR	Belfast and Northern Counties Railway
BR	British Railways
CIE	Coras Iompair Eireann
D&SER	Dublin and South Eastern Railway
E&GR	Edinburgh and Glasgow Railway
GCR	Great Central Railway
GER	Great Eastern Railway
GNR	Great Northern Railway
GNR(I)	Great Northern Railway (Ireland)
GNSR	Great North of Scotland Railway
GSR	Great Southern Railway
GSWR	Great Southern and Western Railway
GWR	Great Western Railway
HR	Highland Railway
LBSCR	London, Brighton and South Coast Railway
LC&DR	London, Chatham and Dover Railway
LMS	London, Midland and Scottish Railway
LNER	London and North Eastern Railway
LNWR	London and North Western Railway
LSWR	London and South Western Railway
LTSR	London, Tilbury and Southend Railway
L&YR	Lancashire and Yorkshire Railway
M&GN	Midland and Great Northern Joint Railway
MGWR	Midland and Great Western Railway
MS&LR	Manchester, Sheffield and Lincolnshire Railway
M&SWJR	Midland and South Western Junction Railway
NBR	North British Railway
NER	North Eastern Railway
NLR	North London Railway
S&DJR	Somerset and Dorset Joint Railway
SECR	South Eastern and Chatham Railway
SER	South Eastern Railway
SR	Southern Railway

Introduction

P. B. Whitehouse

The passing of the Steam Age has left our railways with a new face. Steam itself, the Stephensonic prime mover, made the railways of 150 years ago possible; its power enabled transportation to be swift, cheap and socially acceptable. It also changed and advanced the economic progress not only of Europe and America, but of the world at large. This period of progress, slow to begin with, soon accelerated, surviving two world wars but leaving the railways of Britain in deep financial straits. Salvation meant Grouping and later Nationalisation. Yet in spite of the inevitable entrenchment procedures, like lopping off uneconomic branches, the outward face of the railway itself changed little; stations were solid and sometimes cavernous, signals still stood with their arms replacing those of the old railway policeman, as semaphores, the guard and station inspector checked the time—the railway time—from his pocket watch and the railway horse helped with the shunting as well as with the delivery of parcels. Those were the days of solidarity, when the waiting room chairs were of leather, their backs proudly marked with the owning company's emblem, and the notice which warned you against trespass under a penalty of forty shillings was made of cast iron, sporting the company's name at the top. The great engines had fittings of solid brass—they looked and sounded alive and a proud part of the system to which they belonged.

The coming of the modern railway and the 'new image' put an end to much of this. The motive power became impersonal diesel and electric, signals no longer 'clonked' into position, but were replaced by colour lights. With the building of the big power-controlled boxes, the waistcoated signalman in charge of the shining levers disappeared from the main lines, and stations were 'rationalised' for economic reasons. Anything which was old and which did not fit in with the new thinking was removed. Today we have a system of Inter-City trains. Red Star parcels and container freight trains—we have moved with the times.

Taken as a whole, British railway history has been well recorded: books have been written about most of the companies, large or small, as well as on main lines, branch lines, locomotives, carriages, wagons and station architecture. Museums possess examples of historic engines and vehicles. Preservationists have rescued others and kept some in working order. But how about the 'bits and pieces' the details which make up the whole, what were they and what did they look like? Our larger railway museums have some of these small items on show and hundreds of private enthusiasts have built up their own nostalgic collections which together make up a large part of our railway's historical jigsaw. For if the broad pattern of railway history can be traced in paintings or photographs of great locomotives or famous stations, the details of everyday railway life are evoked by the smaller things, the tickets and labels, the nameplates and number plates, the lamps and whistles, the cutlery, china and glass. Today these pieces of 'railwayana' are collector's items serving an historical purpose, sentimental perhaps, but conjuring up a vanished world.

When and where did this interest start? Probably it all goes back to the publicity put out by the railway companies themselves. Once upon a time every boy wanted to be an engine driver, the hero who controlled those shining, massive, hissing machines which once dominated the world's public transport. From the earliest days, locomotives carried names which fitted the Iron Horse–names like 'Vulcan', 'Firefly', 'Vesuvius' and 'Rocket'–no wonder they caught the imagination. By the beginning of the 20th century, competition and rivalry was such that the publicity side of the business began to receive careful attention, though in that august Edwardian era few would perhaps admit it. The companies started to produce postcards of their locomotives, coaches and lineside views. Led by the London & North Western, which called itself the 'Premier Line', these were sold in their tens of thousands. (The LNW cards originally came in packets of six for twopence.) By the time George V came to the throne, the Great Western Railway was producing its own 'Engine Book' with the classes, names and numbers of its great green machines. The Caledonian sold a magnificent replica of its 'Cardean' and a corridor coach for a few shillings. And so it went on–the lore of the railway was getting a firm foothold.

The next step may well have been the establishment of the learned railway societies, formed principally for the layman. The Stephenson Locomotive Society grew out of the Institution of Locomotive Engineers, and this was followed by the more popular Railway Correspondence and Travel Society. The railway enthusiast became more knowledgable, encouraged both by the companies and by the then few societies which formed the bridge between them. The taker of numbers and the lineside saunterer could, if he wished, become a railway historian.

In the post-war years, the scale of railway enthusiasm mounted rapidly. One indication of this is the success enjoyed by the publishers of railway books. Ian Allan, while working for the Southern Railway, saw the advantage of commercialising the number takers' interest, set up his own company, began to popularise the hobby, and coined the word 'spotter'. His books of names and numbers of the engines of the new Regions of British Railways proved bestsellers almost overnight, and locomotive names became household words. Add to this the demise of the earlier classes of locomotive and the final departure of steam, as well as the British tendency to love that which is not available and it is easy to see where the desire, sometimes sentimental, sometimes avaricious of owning an engine nameplate began in earnest.

Glasgow Central Station, Caledonian Railway, in Edwardian times.

If one looks back, the avalanche started to move in the 1930s, when the older, pre-grouping locomotives were beginning to go to their last rest. In particular, the onslaught made upon London & North Western engines led to their admirers seeking solace in a relic, and what better than a nameplate? The same applied to some of the earlier Great Western classes, for on this well-ordered line standardisation and modernisation were proceeding apace. Hence Crewe could sell you 'Monmouthshire' or 'Hydra', 'Phantom' or 'Sir Ralph Brocklebank' for ten shillings (50p) whilst the Great Western offered 'Saint Helena' or 'Queen Boadicea' for a pound. This situation, plus the Great Western's books at a shilling (5p) for 'Boys of All Ages' and their superb wooden jigsaw puzzles for half a crown (12½p) ensured that a generation was suitably indoctrinated and capable of siring the next and last collectors of steam engine numbers–today's most avid gatherers of railwayana.

Very few people were collecting the 'bits and pieces' of the railway scene for museum purposes during the inter-war years. The larger collections were started when Britain's railways were nationalised and it was clear that much would be swept away with the changing times. Serious enthusiasts, led by the major railway societies campaigned for, and eventually achieved a national railway museum. The Western Region of British Railways (still in their view the GWR), saw to it that a Great Western Museum was established at Swindon as the LNER had done at York in pre-war years, but it was scarcely possible for these excellent organisations to obtain examples of all the smaller relics of the past. A few serious collectors then set out to obtain what they could for their own private museums. At that time so much was being replaced or destroyed with both modernisation and retrenchment that the pickings were there for the asking and superb collections have resulted. One of the finest is in the Midlands and consists of almost everything from a complete set of GWR 'Castle' class motion to luggage labels–all painstakingly collected for the owner's delight and future historical and popular interest. It

Standard engine passes with a difference: the British Transport pass is for locomotive No 1000, the preserved Midland Compound, whilst the CIE pass is for the notorious West Clare line in the west of Ireland. P. B. Whitehouse Collection.

Opposite page:
A selection of wagon plates from the M. V. E. Dunn Collection.
A GWR slip coach tail lamp. Cattell Collection.

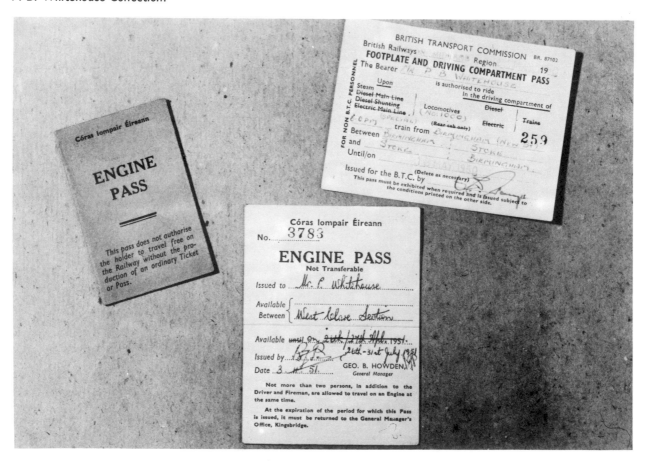

Two fine straps of horse brasses showing different types of early locomotive. These were never issued by the railway companies but were bought by the carters. The left-hand strap contains the brasses of the North Eastern, the London & North Western, the Great Northern and the North Staffordshire Railways. Such company brasses are highly prized and hard to come by. B. Hinchley Collection.

could well have been this collection which sparked off in a Divisional Manager's mind the thought that maybe the nationalised railway was missing something and that a return could be made on the sale of their redundant assets which were being destroyed or given away. Sales were held, relics sold, the avalanche got under way and prices climbed. At the same time cast iron 'trespass' notices on abandoned branch lines–and indeed on lines still in operation–began to disappear rather quickly.

Another way in which the interest in railwayana has been fostered has been with the growth of the tourist or 'preserved' railway and the acquisition of steam locomotives in various shapes, sizes and conditions by private owners. It all began in 1950 with the formation of the world's first railway preservation society in Birmingham–the Talyllyn Railway Preservation Society–which set out to, and obtained control of what was then the world's oldest surviving steam-hauled narrow gauge line. A great deal has been written about this venture and others, so suffice it to say that because it meant adventure, involvement and challenge, the Society succeeded beyond its founders' wildest dreams and has been emulated in various forms the world over. Thus in Britain not only narrow gauge railways, but scenic branches of the British Railways' system have been acquired and operated; these are visited by millions of the general public annually, many of whom have never travelled on a steam train. Each of these organisations, as well as many of the steam 'depots' or collections, seek to restore their own particular museum operation at least to its 'Big Four' face but generally to the pre-grouping era prior to 1923. This has led to a tremendous demand for the bits and pieces of the period to authenticate the operation and thus not only locomotives, coaches and wagons but signals, lamps, notice boards, maps and even cutlery and china have been in fantastic demand. With at least nineteen (at the time of writing) *operating* railways, many more hopefuls and an equal number of private depots or museums, small wonder that many items are in short supply. One should also bear in mind that each organisation has its share (often in hundreds) of volunteer workers who, while keen to acquire items for 'their' railway, also duplicate these for themselves if they can and a rarity situation develops.

By 1969, most of the more glamorous articles had either disappeared or were being bought and sold at enhanced prices. Some, of course, had been carefully sought out and rescued by the National Transport Museum, but dealers, too, were beginning to appear in earnest. During this year, the Stores Controller of the London Midland Region pursuaded his General Manager that even at this late hour there was money

The original photograph by Charles E. Brown which was to form the basis of one of the best known posters of the inter-war years: 'Yes, I always go South for Sunshine by Southern'.

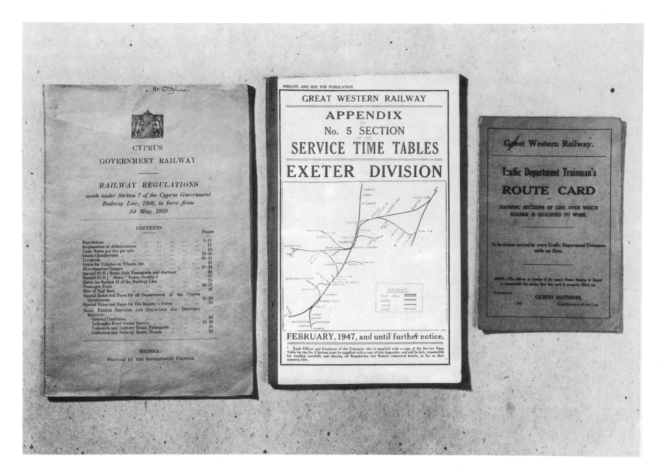

to be made from the sale of what would otherwise have been described as rubbish, and relics of the past once again became respectable. So British Railways became the only state-owned body to run its own second-hand shop, and a profitable one at that. Orders went out throughout the system that anything which could be considered saleable to enthusiasts or collectors must go to London and be sold at a price which the market would bear. Staff from BR's 'Collectors' Corner' visited every nook, cranny and office on the railway to look for a chair with a pre-grouping monogram, a locomotive headlamp to be re-dipped in copper and sold as a decorative 'antique', a piece of redundant signalling apparatus or even the finger-plate of a door–all of these end up at Euston where the saleroom looks like an old warehouse, and even the hardened cynic can find pleasure poking around. Prices are not low, but then they are not meant to be, for this is strictly a business operation. To be fair, 'Collectors' Corner' has a reputation for being just within current market trends and its existence has undoubtedly saved many things from being broken up or burned. One could well exclaim 'if only . . .', for during the '50s and '60s literally tens of thousands of pounds' worth of articles were destroyed which could and would have been avidly collected. These days the BR shop also does its bit for export, for steam and the history of steam is quite big

business and the railway enthusiast and historian have now been joined by the antique trade who have suddenly realised that these relics are part of the heritage of the industrial revolution and are beginning to be regarded as works of art.

Apart from mere acquisitiveness, there is another reason for collecting and that is for the rich fund of knowledge to be gained from a detailed study of certain specified categories of railwayana, such as locomotive works plates, tickets, luggage labels and railway letter stamps. Taking these separately, let us examine some of the information which they can give us.

Works plates can provide data for the historian and lead anyone interested on an enthralling voyage of discovery. In times gone by, the Great Powers of Europe and America have made sure that their industrial firms had orders on their books which would certainly never have arrived there without political pressure. One does not have to look far to find examples. Beginning at home, the old Colonial Empire and even the new Commonwealth purchased most of their railway equipment from the United Kingdom. Companies such as Armstrong Whitworth, Beyer Peacock, Hunslet, Neilson and North British owed their prosperity and even their existence to export sales, and the same applied to American companies like Baldwin and Alco. Plates from locomotives built by these companies can still be found all over the world, showing the works of origin and therefore the base for drawing spares and ultimately heavy repairs. In the case of private manufacturers it was the custom to put the works' construction number on the plate for easy reference.

Tickets can supply other information. For example, there was the Parliamentary ticket when, by means of an Act, every railway company was obliged to run at least one train every day on all of its lines for one penny per mile. Then there was the introduction by the Midland Railway of third class travel on its express trains, or the tickets of soldiers, sailors and shipwrecked mariners as well as tickets which indicated special services, fares or excursions. The study of tickets and timetables alone could occupy a lifetime.

Luggage labels—one of the cheapest collector's items—evoke the days of servants, heavy baggage, 'luggage in advance', porters, cabmen, and problems with changing trains. The Railway Letter Stamp has a railway hobby slant and a philatelic one too. Today it is a source of revenue to certain tourist railways having their own Acts of Parliament dating back to the Railway Letter Act of 1891. As a result of this Act the Postmaster General agreed with the railway companies that they might accept letters for transmission by train provided they bore a suitable postage stamp in addition to a railway letter fare. The letter handed in could either be left at the station to which it was addressed 'to be called for' or posted in the nearest pillar box for delivery by post according to the instructions on the envelope. This service proved a considerable boon in the early days but later became an anachronism. The use of the Railway Letter Stamp was revived in 1957 by the Talyllyn Railway, and this practice has now been followed by other lines. The present-day stamps are decorative and expensive and each new issue becomes a collector's item. Thus railwayana does not necessarily need to be antique to be valuable.

Flare lamps from Melton Constable on the Midland and Great Northern Joint Railway. Cattell Collection.

A 'train following' tail board of either Manchester, Sheffield and Lincoln or the Great Central Railway.

Seekers after relics can still find them with little difficulty, but today, like any asset which has an increasing value as inflation soars, they will not be cheap. Much is done on an exchange basis and the freemasonry of the genuine collector or historian will ensure that those who wish to collect for honourable reasons can obtain their treasures at realistic prices. The beginner or the collector who wishes to invest may well need to approach one of the well known and well tried dealers who advertise in the railway hobby press, or, if he can afford it, attend Christie's or other salerooms for the cream. A visit to one of the 'Open Days' held at steam centres throughout the country during the summer months may provide the opportunity to purchase relics from societies or from individuals who are trying to raise money to save a favourite locomotive or some other worthwhile cause. Such encounters are often rewarding and in any case much of the satisfaction lies in the search.

Each chapter in this book has been written by an expert in his field, a collector who has set out to acquire his items for their historical interest. One cannot hope in one volume, which is the first of its kind, to produce a totally comprehensive survey and space has prevented a detailed study of such specialist areas as horse brasses, railway letter stamps and engine lamps, for example. The field is vast and the detail tantalising. However, if these pages set the seals of intent, then a voyage of further discovery can be undertaken which will bring pleasure and enlightenment to those who embark.

Guards' handlamps, left to right: L&YR, SECR, LSWR, GWR (pre-grouping), GNR, GWR (post-grouping). M. V. E. Dunn Collection.

Publicity literature from four great railway companies. P. B. Whitehouse Collection.

This group of tickets shows some of the many permutations of colour, size, style and design used by the railway companies. The Cook's American Excursions Supplementary Coupon Ticket was issued, along with others, in book form. The Great Northern, Piccadilly & Brompton Railway single journey ticket is interesting for its use of station numbers which are repeated on the reverse. The single weekly ticket of the Buxton Improvement Company is probably the rarest, and certainly the most unusual—it was not issued by a railway company but by a Pavilion Gardens company! Tickets variously from the collections of P. B. Whitehouse, Stuart Underwood, Rev. E. Boston, Michael J. Chapman, John E. Shelbourn and Maurice I. Bray.

Tickets and Passes

Maurice I. Bray

When the railway traveller surrenders his ticket at the barrier he leaves behind a rather commonplace item. Yet the development of that item provides one of the most fascinating and neglected aspects of railway history. In its form of a printed card, it was invented by the Lancashire Quaker, Thomas Edmondson, and was to become the world's standard. What was known to his contemporaries as 'Edmondson's visiting card' was the almost perfect answer to the cumbersome methods of using paper coupon tickets, carried over into the Age of Steam from the stage-coach days.

It is as well to remember that the railways came into operation, not for the conveyance of passengers, but the transport of goods, chiefly coal, and the issue of the first railway ticket is therefore a matter of debate. The original passengers on the early railways were Company guests, formally invited by the Board of Directors. Their fare-paying successors were probably the holders of the first railway tickets; more precisely, they held a printed receipt for their fare. Other travellers on those early railways carried metal tallies which had to be surrendered at the end of a journey. Not until 1838, with the first issue of Edmondson's invention, did the railway ticket as we now recognise it, come into being.

In the days of the staging coach it was essential that the would-be traveller secured a place in the coach at least twenty-four hours prior to the commencement of his journey. Inns of good repute served as 'stations' on the coaching route. Advance booking of a seat was done in an office specially set apart for this purpose at the coaching inn. Not until 1832 did the term 'booking office' come into regular use. In those days a traveller did not merely hand over his money with a request for a ticket to a particular place. A complicated and lengthy process was necessary for the purchase of a ticket. Details of the passenger's name, his destination, the coach in which accommodation was desired, and even his preference for inside or outside travel, were recorded laboriously by hand in triplicate. One copy of this painstakingly produced document was given to the passenger, another to the guard of the coach, while the third was retained as the coaching operator's record. It was not usual for any money to change hands as part of the booking transaction, the fare being paid to the guard at the end of the journey. The pioneer railways carried on this practice of booking a journey. Early railway tickets were of paper, very thin and of inferior quality, each one being handwritten and then cut or torn from a book as required. A full complement of passengers for a staging coach was about twelve persons, so that booking in advance could be accomplished with relative ease. But a train carrying more than a hundred passengers presented quite a different problem. Clearly, a radical change of method was needed in the booking office.

It was on the Leicester and Swannington railway, engineered by Robert Stephenson, that this change was first recorded. Brass octagonal checks or tallies were introduced at the opening of the line in 1832 and were in use until 1846. These new metal tickets, embossed with the initials of the company, a station

Four brass tallies of the old Leicester & Swannington Railway. They were issued to third class passengers who boarded the train according to priority shown by the number. These tallies, provided by the company, were the first break from the cumbersome methods of paper tickets and waybills carried over from the stage coach era. Leicester Museum.

Obverse and reverse of an ivory free pass issued to Mr Farnham. Note the heraldic wyvern which was later used by the Midland Railway. Leicester Museum.

name, and a serial number, were issued in exchange for a fare. This issue permitted admission to the train, and the passenger's priority was indicated by the serial number. At the end of a journey the guard collected the tallies in a special leather pouch for delivery back to the issuing station. The London and Greenwich Railway used circular copper checks, the directors' passes being of silver-bronze carrying a representation of the trans-London Viaduct. Free tickets made of ivory, numbered, and not transferable, were issued by the Sheffield, Ashton-under-Lyne, and Manchester Railway.

But the idea of the metal ticket, although commendable, was a cumbersome and costly alternative to the paper coupon. The metal tally was used in the locomotive sheds, even until comparatively recent times, as a token to be exchanged for wages. The big companies preserved the memory of the metal passenger ticket by issuing gold, silver, or ivory medallions in the style of those early tallies to honoured directors. Free passes, like the directors' medallions, were made of base metal, gold, silver, ivory, parchment, paper and card. In a few instances, notably in Manchester around 1885, xylonite and celluloid were used for tokens to be exchanged for tickets. Ornate parchment passes were issued for first class travel. They died out for economic reasons, it being cheaper to print on card or paper which was then mounted in a gold-blocked leather cover. It is difficult to differentiate between passes, certain types of Season tickets and the ultimate issue of Privilege tickets. Free passes and Privilege tickets were, and still are, issued to company servants, their families, and company guests. Their average period of validity was seven days, and like standard issues, they were not transferable.

After a varied career, ranging from apprentice cabinet-maker to grocer, Thomas Edmondson was appointed station master at Milton (later Brampton Junction) on the Newcastle and Carlisle Railway. It was not long before he recognised the disadvantages in the existing ticket issuing system. Being of an inventive nature he gave considerable thought to the problem and evolved a new system whereby the passengers were identified by number instead of by name. For this system he used a wooden matrix inset with type giving station names and classes. With the wooden block and a mallet he printed rows and rows of tickets upon some suitably textured and coloured card. After the laborious addition of a serial number to each ticket they were cut out of the cardboard strip and placed in a special box ready for issue. There was a marked improvement in speed with which tickets were issued but Edmondson was not yet satisfied. He next developed the ticket tube in which the pre-printed cards were stored in numerical order. Removal of the uppermost ticket allowed the remainder to

Metal countermarks, tokens and passes have a complex and interwoven history. Some were minted in the form of coins, those of elaborate design on precious metal being reserved for use as directors' free passes. The brass tokens illustrated here were used as duty checks and as pay checks to establish identity when taking receipt of a pay packet. Stuart Underwood Collection.

ascend, controlled by a counter-balanced plate, leaving the next ticket ready for issue. Edmondson also contrived a ticket-dating press, the ticket being gripped between two movable jaws. The drawback was that the jaws were unprotected and therefore dangerous; later models were improved upon by Edmondson's son in 1862.

Edmondson's ticket dating press. National Railway Museum.

OPENING
OF
The Leicester and Swannington
RAILWAY,
Tuesday, 17th July, 1832.

The Bearer of this Ticket is entitled to Seat, No. *111* in
Carriage No. *4* Entered *John Eles*

COCKSHAW, PRINTER.

Opening day ticket of the Leicester and Swannington Railway. To judge by the number, the carriages must have been crowded indeed. Leicester Museum.

A first class free pass disc.

Railway tickets as we have now come to know them, were first formally adopted on the Birmingham and Gloucester line. Their advantages became publicly known, and eventually Edmondson's tickets and machines were to be found in every booking office. During the years of the ticket's development variations on the standard were to be found throughout the railway world. While many countries adopted Edmondson's ticket dimensions, others, while retaining his ticket-issuing system, preferred their own style of ticket. Instead of a coloured card measuring $2\frac{1}{4}$in by $1\frac{3}{16}$in several European lines issued tickets which measured a mere $1\frac{1}{2}$in by $\frac{5}{8}$in. One of the largest railway tickets was that issued by the Persian State Railway, measuring 8in by 4in. Circular tickets were a rarity, but during 1935 were in use in what was then British North Borneo; in more recent times they have been issued, notably in 1970, with the British Rail Games Rover Ticket which allowed period travel in Scotland during the Commonwealth Games.

The use of colour was the next innovation. Many of the railway companies' employees could not read and so the best means of enabling them to distinguish tickets of different categories was by the use of various colours. Early issues show that the use of colour was kept to a minimum, the most popular range being white for first class, pink for second, and green for third. But events on the 5th July, 1841, changed all

This ticket blank shows that, despite Edmondson's invention of almost thirty years earlier, one company still preferred to use the old coaching style ticket. P. B. Whitehouse Collection.

that. On the morning of that day a Midland Counties locomotive and train steamed out of Leicester station en route for Loughborough, some twelve miles distant. It was the world's first publicly advertised excursion train, a highly successful venture, the effects of which spread far and wide. The railway companies began to look into the potential of the excursion business, so as to expand their already fast increasing and popular services. Because of the many and varied services which the companies offered, the ticket range had to be extended, and more tickets meant more colours. It was not unusual for several permutations of at least seven different colours to be used on a company's tickets. Some were half white and half yellow, red and blue, or buff and green, while other tickets were available with a strip of one colour crossing one or more other colours. As many as seven alternating bands of colour printed onto one ticket was not uncommon. Distinctive colours tended to be used for excursion trains, with further permutations of colour for the various classes. 'Down line' trains were accorded different colours from the 'up line'. It was quite a common practice on all the railways to organise excursions on successive days. By the issue of a different coloured ticket each day, the collector or the examiner was able to tell at a glance that the ticket handed to him was the correct one for that day.

Special tickets were a nightmare to the booking-clerks and the examiners and their lot was not made easier by the ever-present threat of forgery and fare evasion. Confusion was even more confounded with the issue at some stations of Market tickets, or Day Picnic tickets, which were merely ordinary day tickets with an appropriate overprint. In an attempt to counter ticket forgers the Great Western Railway in 1928 adopted bank-note style printing for season tickets. The idea was two-fold: to safeguard both the company and the public by the use of an ingenious design and to produce an attractive ticket which would maintain their reputation as promoters of fine art. The process of printing from steel engravings was perfected by Messrs Thomas de la Rue for the new Bank of England notes, and the quality of the work they did for railway season tickets was equally fine. Especially noticeable are the delicate details of the company's crest which occupied a prominent position in the design. An alternative to the bank-note style of printing was the 'safety background'. This was usually printed in a contrasting colour to that of the base card, and consisted of a repeated geometric design, the company's crest or monogram worked into a continuous pattern, or simply the company's initials repeated in a fine type-face to make a continuous background.

24

But every one of these chromo-lithographed or offset printed tickets, however decorative, had to be issued. By the early 1930s, the world's railway companies were printing tickets in such staggering numbers that serious thought had to be given to the problems of storage and issue. The tremendous advantages of self-printed tickets became evident to those engaged upon research into the problem. The threat of fraud was removed, accountancy and audit checks were simplified, and considerable economies could be effected in production costs.

Ticket machines then began to appear in booking offices. One example, extensively used in Britain and Europe, was the A.E.G. Multi–Printer manufactured in Germany. The cast-iron underframe carried a magazine which could house as many as 2,500 printing plates. Although the machines produced the Edmondson standard size, only card roll of a single colour could be used. This meant that the tickets so produced had to look entirely different from any others in the company's galaxy of cards. The type-face had to indicate the usual category details in an easily read aspect. The reference to company regulations also had to appear among the destination and fare details. As many as fifteen separate items could be listed on a single ticket where the company operated a zone system. Together with printing identification marks, this made for a rather crowded ticket face.

The London Underground stands supreme as one of the world's pioneers of the use of mechanical aids in the booking office. In 1904 a coin-slot machine with a pull bar operated by the passenger, and issuing ready-printed tickets, was installed on the Central London line. Four years later an electrically operated machine was in use. Another early device was the passimeter, a form of turnstile–cum–ticket machine. Upon insertion of the appropriate coin, the machine dated, cancelled, and issued a ticket. Subsequent action of the machine freed the flapper-arm of the turnstile which was automatically re-set after the passenger had negotiated the turnstile.

The many types of passenger ticket used by the different companies may be placed in five main groups, viz: Ordinary Tickets, Tourist Tickets, Cheap Ordinary Tickets, Excursion Tickets, Season or Contract Tickets.

LMS special ticket, probably early 1930s. The left-hand edge is perforated, indicating that it was contained within a book. Tickets like these were issued to wartime evacuees. Stuart Underwood Collection.

79512

L. M. & S. RAILWAY   SPECIAL TICKET

NOT TRANSFERABLE.

AVAILABLE FOR ONE PERSON ON DAY OF ISSUE ONLY. TO BE RETAINED UNTIL COMPLETION OF JOURNEY.

FROM STATION OF ISSUE BY

L. M. & S. RLY. TRAIN

AND THENCE TO FINAL DESTINATION

THE STRICT CONDITION OF THE ISSUE OF THIS TICKET IS THAT THE HOLDER SHALL COMPLY WITH ALL INSTRUCTIONS GIVEN BY OFFICIALS.

ISSUED SUBJECT TO BYE-LAWS, REGULATIONS AND CONDITIONS OF THE RAILWAYS

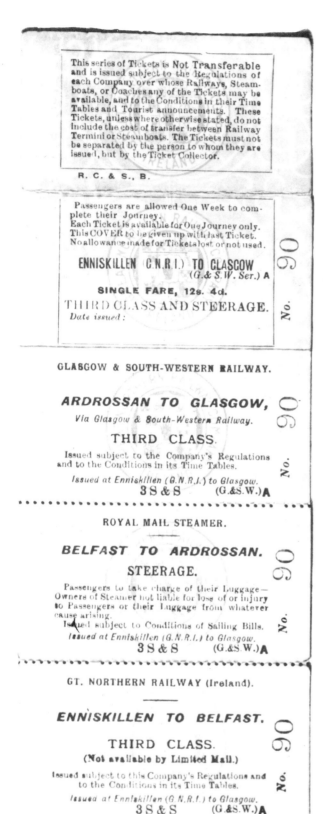

Passengers are allowed One Week to complete their Journey.
Each Ticket is available for One Journey only.
This COVER to be given up with last Ticket.
No allowance made for Tickets lost or not used.

ENNISKILLEN (G.N.R.I.) TO GLASGOW
(G. & S. W. Ser.) A

SINGLE FARE, 12s. 4d.

THIRD CLASS AND STEERAGE.
Date issued :

No. 90

GLASGOW & SOUTH-WESTERN RAILWAY.

ARDROSSAN TO GLASGOW,
Via Glasgow & South-Western Railway.

THIRD CLASS.

Issued subject to the Company's Regulations and to the Conditions in its Time Tables.
Issued at Enniskillen (G.N.R.I.) to Glasgow.
3 S & S   (G.&S.W.) A

No. 90

ROYAL MAIL STEAMER.

BELFAST TO ARDROSSAN.

STEERAGE.

Passengers to take charge of their Luggage— Owners of Steamer not liable for loss of or injury to Passengers or their Luggage from whatever cause arising.
Issued subject to Conditions of Sailing Bills.
Issued at Enniskillen (G.N.R.I.) to Glasgow.
3 S & S   (G.&S.W.) A

No. 90

GT. NORTHERN RAILWAY (Ireland).

ENNISKILLEN TO BELFAST.

THIRD CLASS.
(Not available by Limited Mail.)

Issued subject to this Company's Regulations and to the Conditions in its Time Tables.
Issued at Enniskillen (G.N.R.I.) to Glasgow.
3 S & S   (G.&S.W.) A

No. 90

GNR (Ireland) and Glasgow & South Western Railway joint issue multi-stage coupon ticket. P. B. Whitehouse Collection.

Ordinary Tickets

Although each company was empowered at its foundation (in Britain, by Parliamentary sanction) to charge reasonable fares, the sums varied considerably between the companies, ranging in 1855 from 3d to 9d for certain first class fares. Further differences were determined by the type of travel, ie express or ordinary train. Generally, fares in Britain were charged upon a distance travelled basis, but after the Government assumption of control of the railways in 1914, the fare structures underwent radical alterations. From the beginning, no Railway Act had ever required a company to issue return tickets, but the companies found that fare reductions tended to bring about an increase in passenger traffic. Special conditions were operated with the issue of Ordinary tickets, such conditions being printed, or referred to, somewhere on the ticket, usually on the reverse. As a general rule, Ordinary singles and outward halves of Ordinary returns were available on the day of issue only. Considerable support was given to the proposal that tickets should be issued without time limitations, and to this end several unsuccessful Bills were placed before Parliament.

Tourist Tickets

This category, not to be confused with Cheap Ordinary tickets, was originally a special issue for the convenience of passengers on tour. Such passengers had the right to break their journey, usually at specified stations, the tickets being valid for periods of one week, and more. As long ago as 1852, a ticket for travel to Ireland was valid for one month; by 1916, when the issue of Tourist tickets was suspended, the period of validity had been extended to six months. Subsequent re-issue in 1921 imposed a two months' limit. Originally, Tourist tickets had been intended for first class passengers only with a charge of single fare and a half. Later increased to single fare and three-quarters, they were generally introduced in 1872 and the third class fares were adjusted accordingly. The first major fare revision for Tourist tickets was in 1900, part of an overall re-structuring of fare schedules. The second revision, a 5% increase on third class tourist fares, was caused by the after effects of the 1911 rail strike. Tourist ticket issues were initially restricted to the summer season, but were gradually extended into the winter months. Agreement was reached between the companies that Tourist tickets should only be issued to 'Recognised Tourist Resorts'. The addition of a resort to a company's published list had to be approved by the Railway Clearing House at an annual meeting.

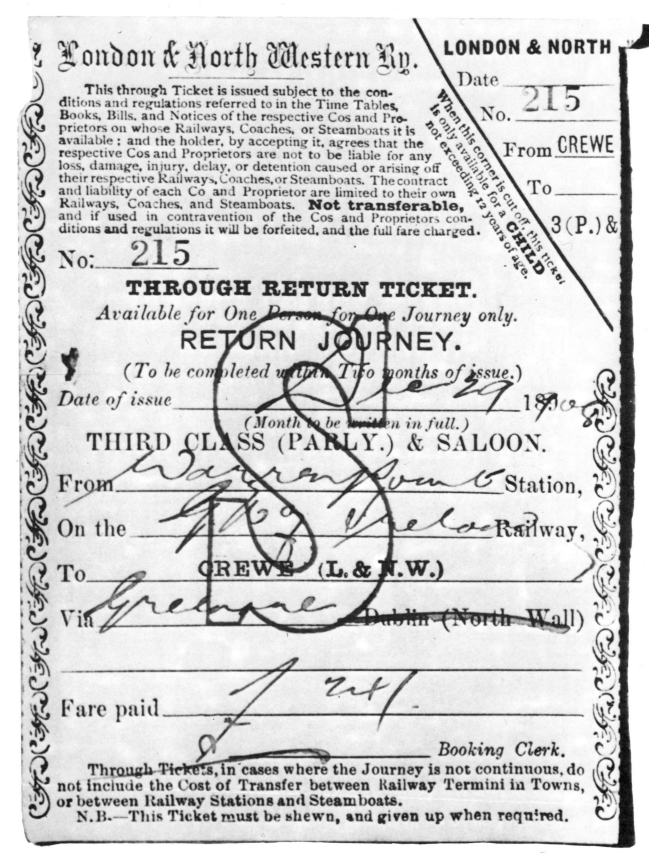

London & North Western Ry.

This through Ticket is issued subject to the conditions and regulations referred to in the Time Tables, Books, Bills, and Notices of the respective Cos and Proprietors on whose Railways, Coaches, or Steamboats it is available ; and the holder, by accepting it, agrees that the respective Cos and Proprietors are not to be liable for any loss, damage, injury, delay, or detention caused or arising off their respective Railways, Coaches, or Steamboats. The contract and liability of each Co and Proprietor are limited to their own Railways, Coaches, and Steamboats. **Not transferable,** and if used in contravention of the Cos and Proprietors conditions and regulations it will be forfeited, and the full fare charged.

No: **215**

THROUGH RETURN TICKET.

Available for One Person for One Journey only.

RETURN JOURNEY.

(To be completed within Two months of issue.)

Date of issue _____ 1890

(Month to be written in full.)

THIRD CLASS (PARLY.) & SALOON.

From _____ Station,

On the _____ Railway,

To **CREWE (L. & N.W.)**

Via _____ Dublin (North Wall)

Fare paid _____

_____ Booking Clerk.

Through Tickets, in cases where the Journey is not continuous, do not include the Cost of Transfer between Railway Termini in Towns, or between Railway Stations and Steamboats.

N.B.—This Ticket must be shewn, and given up when required.

LONDON & NORTH

Date _____

No. **215**

From **CREWE**

To _____

3 (P.) &

When this corner is cut off, this ticket is only available for a **CHILD** not exceeding 12 years of age.

LNWR third class 'Parly' and Saloon return ticket.
P. B. Whitehouse Collection.

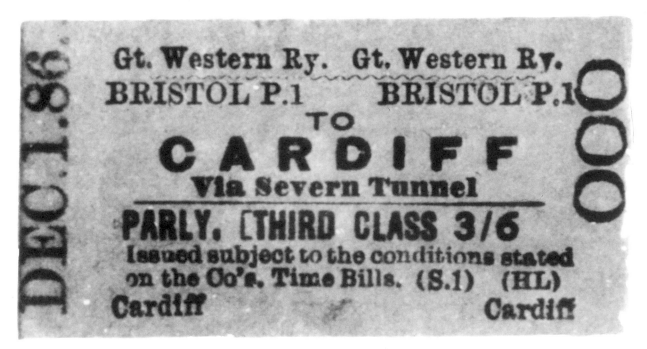

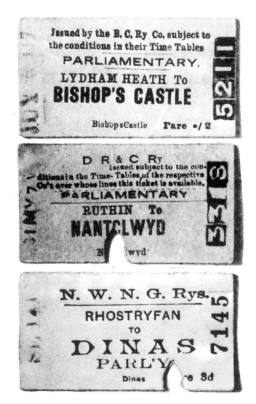

GWR third class 'Parly' ticket. Green. This is an historic ticket, being the first to be issued by the GWR for the Bristol to Cardiff journey via the Severn Tunnel, completed in 1886 at a cost of two million pounds. P. B. Whitehouse Collection.

Three 'Parliamentary' tickets issued respectively by Bishop's Castle Railway Company, the Denbigh Ruthin & Corwen and the North Wales Narrow Gauge Railways. P. B. Whitehouse Collection.

Cheap Ordinary Tickets
During the Government control of the railways in Britain, many cheap travelling concessions were withdrawn. By order of the Railway Executive Committee, from March, 1915, and until further notice, withdrawal of Excursion and Cheap Fare Facilities was effected. These and other restrictions had less than the desired effect in reducing passenger traffic. Upon the lifting of the restrictions an almost endless variety of cheap fare concessions was made available. The by now re-grouped British railways catered for everybody from anglers to strolling players, bell ringers to shipwrecked mariners, concert parties to battlefield pilgrims, even paupers on the Great Western. The conditional issue of the Cheap Ordinary tickets was aimed at increasing traffic, with each of the 'Big Four' launching widespread advertising campaigns. Special Week-End tickets were made available for all classes of passengers. Issued at a single fare and a third for a return journey, these tickets were available between specified times, and with conditions relating to the amount of free luggage which could be carried. Certain types of Week-End tickets were issued as combined rail and hotel tickets, and for an inclusive charge passengers could stay with full board at a high-class hotel. It is almost impossible to draw a distinction between the Tourist ticket and the ultimate development of the Cheap Ordinary ticket. Diverse facilities enabled passengers to travel to one station, and return from another by ordinary trains, usually within territorial limits of 60 miles radius from the station of departure. Tickets were issued at one half the ordinary single fare, and were available over different periods.

A group of tickets issued respectively by Great Western and London joint lines; Macclesfield Committee; Cheshire Lines Committee; Midland & Great Northern Joint; London and North Western; London, Chatham & Dover and London and North Western. The Midland & Great Northern furlough ticket is of a type issued by Statute to members of the armed forces and to policemen who paid approximately three-quarters of the ordinary fare. The Macclesfield Committee first class single had to wait until 1967 before it was issued. Tickets variously in the collections of the Rev E. Boston and Maurice I. Bray.

02886 Weston, Clevedon & Portishead Railway second class single issued in 1906. P. B. Whitehouse Collection. 023 LMS third class single 'pull-out' advertisement ticket blank. M. J. Chapman Collection. 0218 Southern Railway Isle of Wight cruise ticket, unissued, buff card with green band overprint. J. E. Shelbourn Collection. 299 GWR half-day excursion, first class, unissued.

Horizontal pink band on white card. J. E. Shelbourn Collection. 2995 Midland Railway fourth class single, probably c. 1865. Buff. J. E. Shelbourn Collection. 1690 Oxford, Worcester & Wolverhampton second class single issued in April, 1911. Dark blue. Stuart Underwood Collection.

Excursion Tickets

The Excursion ticket has generally been defined as a form of Cheap Ordinary ticket issued usually in connection with the running of special trains. As always, its period of validity can range from half-day to a long period; infringement of any of the advertised conditions of issue have generally required the passenger to pay the full ordinary fare. Bright colours, pre-printed date of issue, and shape and size differing from the Edmondson standard, have always been a predominant feature of Excursion tickets. It was not unusual for the numbers of special excursion trains to be printed on the ticket along with the time schedules.

Season or Contract Tickets

Where passengers travelled daily on standard services, companies accorded them the privilege of purchasing a Season or Contract ticket, the rates being low. Most holders of Season tickets, then as now, made one round journey per day, although it is not unknown for more frequent use to have been made. Special half-price Seasons were available to persons between the ages of 12 and 18. Some companies granted further reductions in the charge where two or more Seasons were purchased by members of the same family, but with the standardisation of the issue of Seasons in 1918, such rather extravagant concessions were withdrawn.

Season tickets were a very early development on British railways, and were originally known as 'Periodical Tickets'. During the 1850s, many of the companies, on their lines north-bound out of London, offered a free first class Season to anyone erecting new buildings in residential land adjoining the railways. These gratuitous tickets were eagerly sought, since they were valid for periods up to twenty years. In 1852 the London and South Western Railway introduced Residential tickets for the occupiers of houses in these encouraged developments; they were issued at a 20% discount for a period of seven years. Conditions of issue for Seasons have always been much more varied and complex than for most other types of ticket. The basic condition has always been that it is not transferable and can be used on any ordinary service train. Stations of departure and destinations are listed, together with further conditions relating to its validity.

A less familiar version of the Season was that issued to traders whose traffic over a company's metals equalled a nominal financial amount per annum. The concession of one ticket was granted, and more tickets would be issued for an annually sustained traffic, the value of which was in multiples of that amount. This category of ticket remained virtually unchanged, until, after nationalisation, an All-Regions Runabout ticket was introduced. The fare was

Midland Railway first class season ticket (actual size), personally signed by the General Manager, James Allport. The year of issue, 1866, was printed in red on both halves of the ticket. George Dow Collection.

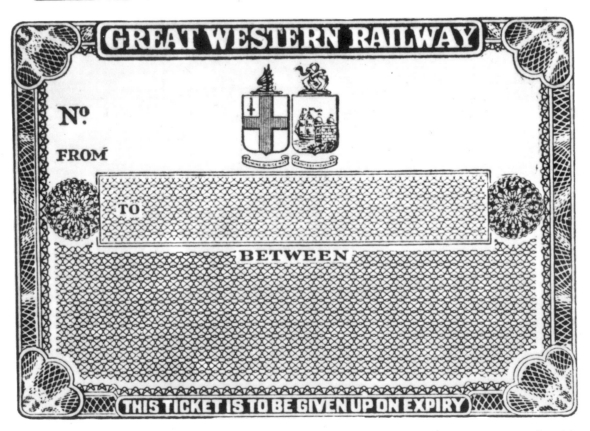

Stockton & Darlington Railway.

SEASON TICKET.

First Class.

To Mr. _____

DARLINGTON AND REDCAR.

From the _____ day of _____ inclusive,

to _____ day of _____ inclusive.

_____ Secretary.

_____

The holder of this Ticket is subject to the same Rules and Regulations as other Passengers.

GREAT WESTERN RAILWAY

Nᵒ

FROM

TO

BETWEEN

THIS TICKET IS TO BE GIVEN UP ON EXPIRY

Stockton & Darlington Railway first class season ticket blank. Pink card. Date unknown, but certainly prior to 1865. J. E. Shelbourn Collection.

GWR season ticket blank of the type introduced by that company in 1928. Maurice I. Bray Collection. (Both tickets are shown enlarged.)

around £600 for first class and £400 for second class; the scheme proved to be uneconomical so it was scrapped. To replace the Runabout a 'new' type of ticket was introduced, known as a ticket by Arranged Contract, very little different from the original Traders' Season. Much publicity was given in 1972 to the purchase by two London businessmen of Arranged Contract tickets which cost £842.40 each. The special gold-lettered tickets were issued at Euston.

Other Tickets and Ticket Systems

A well-known category of railway ticket was the Workman's ticket, which had its origins in the Cheap Trains Act of 1844. This Act provided that every railway company had to run at least one train per day, by which third class passengers were carried for fares not exceeding one penny per mile. The ticket issued for such a journey was labelled simply as 'Parliamentary' with no reference to class. The effect of the Cheap Trains Act of 1883 was that railway companies were no longer required to run 'Parly' trains. Instead, they had to provide a proportional increase in third class accommodation, and became obliged to provide workmen's trains. Despite the revisions recommended by the Rates Advisory Committee in 1920, workmen's trains were uneconomic. In advising that the term was neither practical nor desirable of definition, the 1920 Committee recommended that the workmen's trains be known as 'Cheap Early Trains', a suggestion which was adopted by all the principal companies.

It is generally accepted that a ticket is a receipt for the fare that has been paid, and also an agreement by the company to carry the passenger safely between the stations named. A contract is two-sided with implied obligations, and although there is little on the face of a ticket to indicate such a contract, there is usually some reference to conditions to be found elsewhere. Such a reference, with slight variations, reads: 'This Ticket is issued subject to the Regulations and Conditions stated in the Company's Time Tables and Bills.' Although the passenger could truthfully claim that he knew nothing of any conditions, it has been generally established in law that where conditions, or references thereto, are actually printed on a ticket, they become binding. Special tickets which induced the passenger to waive his rights to compensation (notably the Workman's ticket) were negated by the purchase of an Insurance ticket. For as little as twopence, being in effect an insurance policy, they guaranteed as much as £500 in the case of death, or £3 per week for life where permanent injury occurred. Double these benefits could be obtained with the purchase of a 6d Insurance ticket for a return journey.

Another type of ticket which had a brief reign in the 1930s was the advertisement card, similar in design to the Insurance ticket. Essentially, the ticket was made of two thin cards cut to Edmondson's standard, and glued together to form a pocket. A small finger notch was cut into the top edges and a tiny advertisement card, measuring approximately 1½in by ⅞in, was slotted into the pocket. It was not too popular, on either side of the booking-office window. Apart from its increased bulk, with the obvious restrictions on storage, it also presented problems in the Clearing Houses. Advertisements had been printed onto the backs of Edmondson's tickets issued by the Great Western Railway in 1871, but the idea was not a great success. A ticket remains a relatively short time in the holder's possession, so that it was exceptional to find advertisements on railway tickets.

Finally, mention should be made of the Platform ticket. Introduced to Britain from the Continent, it has had its detractors who claim that it encouraged fraud, though various elaborate attempts have been made to prevent abuses.

An important milestone in railway ticket history was the formation of the Railway Clearing House. In the early days of railways there was no provision for through booking, and passengers had to suffer the inconveniences of changing trains even on short journeys. The establishment of the Clearing House in 1842 helped to solve the problem of who was to receive the money, and in what proportion, when a traveller bought a ticket from one company and journeyed to a station served by another. The early difficulties which beset the Clearing House lay in the bewildering variety of shapes, sizes, colours, and materials of the tickets. By the year 1851, Clearing House staff were sorting through more than 12,000 tickets per week. It says much for the administration and the staff, that throughout its entire history there were few perceptible discrepancies in the vast balance sheets.

Since the beginning of the railways as a commercial venture, many systems have been evolved to account for the movements of passengers and the resultant revenue. The ticket has proved supreme in this field, and yet its final form has still to be decided. New developments in the system of ticket issue have brought the unpretentious card full circle. Paper coupon tickets with a safety background, and continuous roll tickets printed and issued instanter, are but modern descendants of the issues of the 1920s and the new ticket systems are electronic echoes of the mechanical systems introduced on the London Underground more than fifty years ago. Whatever the final development of the ticket system, the network of iron roads will always have a romantic and colourful history firmly anchored in the tiny slip of pasteboard.

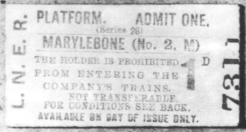

A group of platform tickets. 0183 Kingston upon Hull Corporation Pier admission ticket, issued by the LNER, 1934. Rev. E. Boston Collection. 1530 LNER ticket, c. 1930, the linear clock being punched in the appropriate time space upon issue. Stuart Underwood Collection. 0736 A typical GWR ticket of the mid-1930s. M. J. Chapman Collection. 3366 An unusual LMS ticket which allowed non-travellers to enter the station premises to make use of the station dining room. M. J. Chapman Collection. 7311 LNER ticket, the details printed in red with the serial number in black. P. B. Whitehouse Collection. 28 An unusual Great Eastern ticket made of pressed brass with the letters and serial number space in relief against a black enamel ground. P. B. Whitehouse Collection.

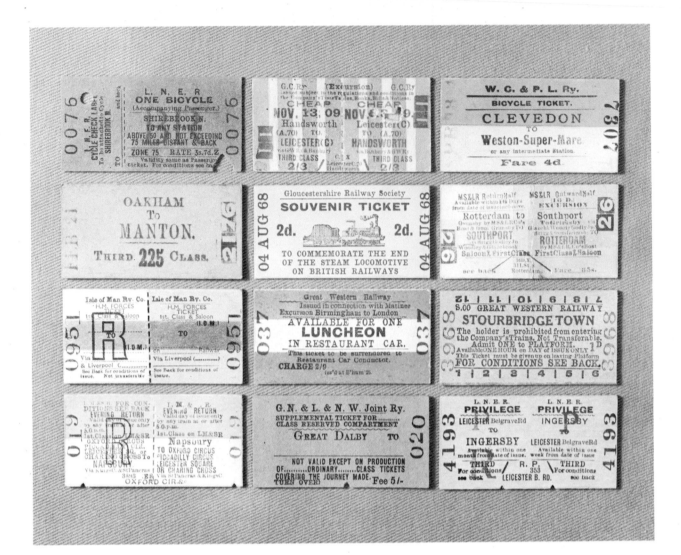

A colourful array of tickets, spanning nearly a hundred years. The souvenir ticket of the Gloucestershire Railway Society tells its own sorry tale. The Great Central Railway cheap excursion ticket is a good example of the elaborate measures used to thwart forgers and fare dodgers—the reverse is coloured lilac as a further safeguard. The GWR platform ticket had to wait nearly eighteen years before it was issued. A familiar Great Western style is depicted with the luncheon ticket. The Manchester, Sheffield & Lincolnshire Railway 16-days excursion was never issued. To judge by the series number, few people were interested in a trip to Rotterdam, first class, for thirty-five shillings. Tickets variously from the collections of Michael J. Chapman, Rev. E. Boston, Maurice I. Bray and P. B. Whitehouse.

A ticket issued on the famous Stockton & Darlington Railway and bearing the signature of the 'Father of the Railways', George Stephenson. It would appear to have been issued for use as a Pass Ticket, since the destination details on the face have been cancelled along with the ticket number. The original category was Government Class. Chesterfield Museum.

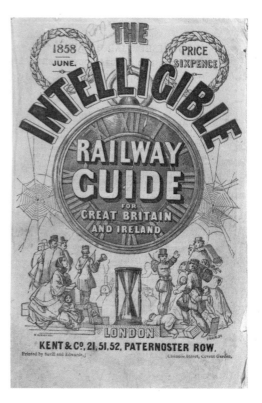

Cover of The Intelligible Railway Guide *for June, 1858.*
Jeoffry Spence Collection.
A group of timetable covers. The Lancashire, Derbyshire and East Coast Railway example is for 1879. Murray's Scottish timetable was issued quarterly from 1842 and monthly from April, 1845 — the number illustrated is for January, 1915. Thurnham's ABC is also dated January, 1915. The blue cover is the reverse of Reid's Railway and Post Guide for January, 1918, and the regular ABC is for April 1919. C. M. Whitehouse Collection.

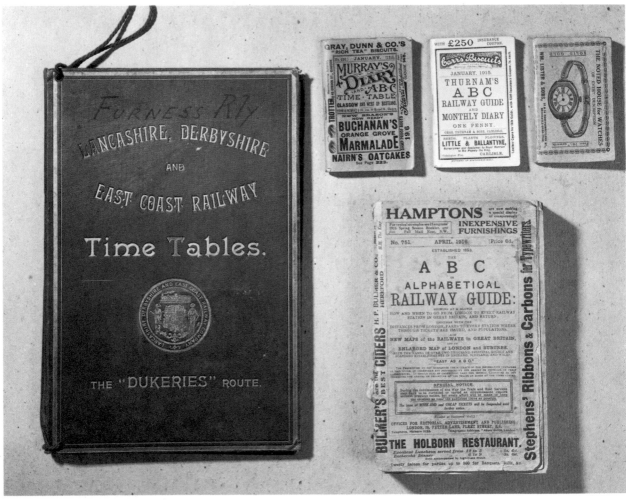

Timetables

Jeoffry Spence

For the devotee of the railway timetable the 'best' route could mean anything from the shortest time between two given points to the scenic route with three changes—and at least an hour's wait at one of them. Times have changed, and there is no longer the variety of routes to complicate and confuse the uninitiated. In fact, timetables have lost a lot of their glamour. Even the British Railways' new massive timetable, with symbols of crossed knife and fork for a full meal service, or a pitchfork in a circle which indicates 'Buffet service of a hot dish to order . . . ' is disappointingly easy to follow, for it lasts for a whole year instead of the old idea of a monthly issue.

It appears that the first timetable, (other than timesheets which had been published since coaching days) was that produced by James Drake of Birmingham in July 1838. This showed the times of trains between Euston and the temporary terminus at Denbigh Hall near Bletchley, the road connexions to Rugby, the trains from Rugby to Birmingham, and the trains of the Grand Junction and Liverpool & Manchester Railways. Drake's timetables did not apparently last very long.

Of all the timetables that have appeared over the years the undoubted classic is Bradshaw's 'Guide'. George Bradshaw was born on 29 July 1801 at Windsor Bridge, Pendleton, near Salford and, on leaving school, became an engraver, particularly of maps. He engaged in letterpress printing with a partner, William T. Blacklock, thus forming the firm of Bradshaw & Blacklock, which later became Henry Blacklock & Co Ltd.

Bradshaw died on 6 September 1853 of cholera, which he contracted when on a visit to Norway, and is buried in Oslo.

There is evidence that Bradshaw started a timetable as early as 1838, but this was virtually a local affair. His first guide was that dated October 1839. Number 1, dated 19 October, was of the northern railways only; number 2 was dated 25 October and was for the southern railways. Number 3 was also dated 25 October and was the first national guide, being a combination of numbers 1 and 2. It will be observed that the name of the month was not shown, for Bradshaw was a Quaker, and the Society of Friends did not approve of pagan names in the calendar. The actual date was shown as 10th Mo. 19th, 1839.

Bradshaw's first 'Railway Guide', the forerunner of the famous guide, was published in December 1841 and, despite religious scruples, was actually shown as 'For December 1841'. There is one extant copy preserved at the Bodleian Library in Oxford. It measures approximately 6in by 4¾in and was produced with dull yellow wrappers, a colour which continued to be used until the First World War when it was replaced by a drab white. In 1932 a certain amount of red typeface was used on the covers, which brightened them up a little. 1939 was the centenary year, and from May the cover became gold, blue and cream. Blacklock's proposed that the October issue—the centenary month —should have covers of gold, red and blue, but the outbreak of war upset these plans. October appeared in red and white, which it retained to the very end.

Cover of Bradshaw's Railway Guide *for December, 1841. Bodleian Library.*

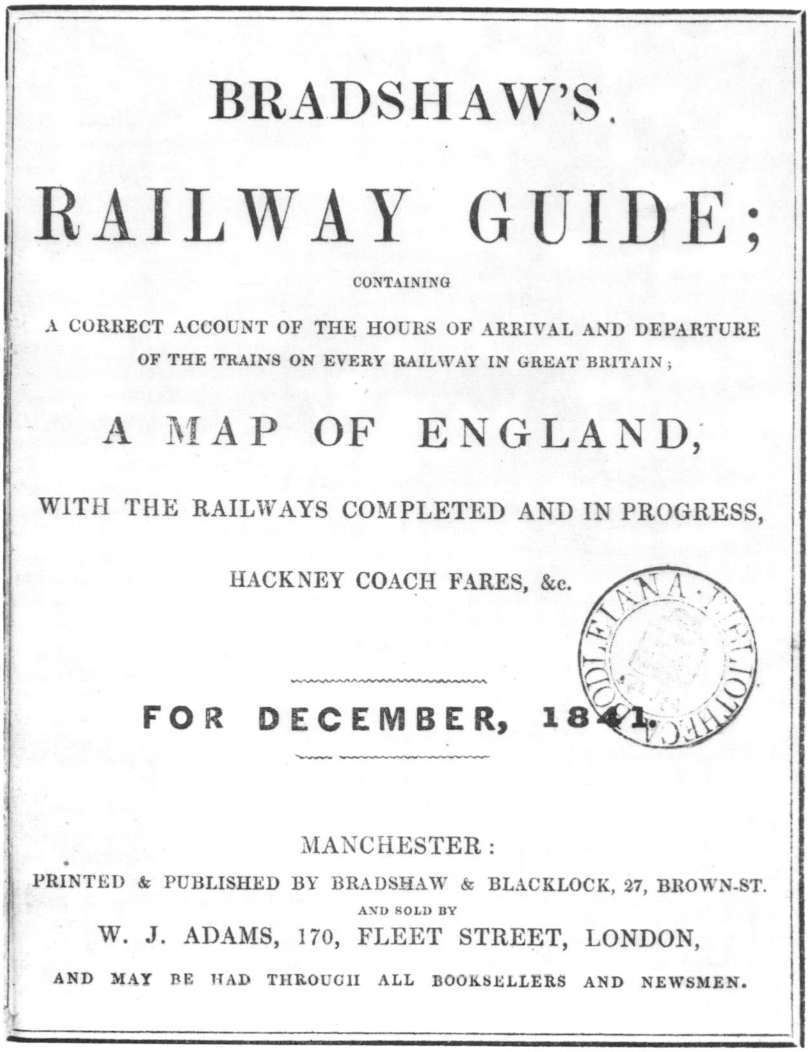

BRADSHAW'S.

RAILWAY GUIDE;

CONTAINING

A CORRECT ACCOUNT OF THE HOURS OF ARRIVAL AND DEPARTURE OF THE TRAINS ON EVERY RAILWAY IN GREAT BRITAIN;

A MAP OF ENGLAND,

WITH THE RAILWAYS COMPLETED AND IN PROGRESS,

HACKNEY COACH FARES, &c.

FOR DECEMBER, 1841.

MANCHESTER:

PRINTED & PUBLISHED BY BRADSHAW & BLACKLOCK, 27, BROWN-ST.

AND SOLD BY

W. J. ADAMS, 170, FLEET STREET, LONDON,

AND MAY BE HAD THROUGH ALL BOOKSELLERS AND NEWSMEN.

From January 1842 Bradshaw conceded a small point to the more ignorant or more heathen population and showed the date as 'No. II. 1st Mo. (January) 1842'. This method of presentation lasted to the end if an entire month was shown, but from the early 1920s the complications which arose from summer and winter timetables starting during the course of a month caused them to adopt the more usual form eg '10th JULY 1922', 'AUGUST to SEPTEMBER 11th, 1932', 'From JULY 6th 1936'. For the first few years train times were shown as a.m. and p.m. in the normal way, but in about 1848 the abbreviations 'mrn.' and 'aft.' were given, and this persisted right up to about a year or so after the last war, when it reverted to a.m. and p.m. There were other idiosyncracies about *Bradshaw*. The best known was the addition of 100 to the serial number: March 1845 was correctly numbered 40, but the April 1845 issue was numbered 141. This error was never corrected, and one of the *Bradshaw* experts, the late Canon Reginald Fellows, thinks it was a deliberate mistake to make it appear more thoroughly established than it really was.

Bradshaw's index to stations was not particularly helpful in early days, when only the main stations were listed. With the increase in the opening of lines the index also increased, but it was not until 1856 that all stations were shown. Presumably in order to economise, the size of type was reduced which, together with the fact that the paper used was not of very good quality must have made it difficult for elderly eyes and even bad for young ones. An improvement in type-face for the index was not effected until 1909 when the whole thing became more legible.

Bradshaw has had its rough periods, particularly during the early 1870s when, doubtless again due to increase in traffic and more trains, the publishers, trying to keep down any increase in the size of the guide, crammed too much into too little space, resulting in a general untidiness, hands pointing in all directions in the train columns, with tiny tables tucked away upside down in odd corners. Even in the 1880s things had not improved much, and such appalling abbreviations of station names appeared as shown opposite in a London & South Western table:

Raynes P.
WrcstrPk.
Ewell [77
Epsm †75
Ashtd [60
Lethrhd ‡

Cmbe & Ml
Srbtn [dn

Page 77 referred to another service at Epsom, and 60 to that at Leatherhead. ‡ meant 'Station for Bookham, Effingham and Horsley'.

The *Bradshaw* notes were always bewildering, and their station nomenclature often vague, but an attempt was sometimes made to help the passenger by telling him that, for instance, Clapham Junction was 'Mid-Battersea; 1¼ miles to Clapham', or that at Wickham Market on the Great Eastern the station was '2 miles distant at Campsea Ash'. It is believed that many of these notes were *Bradshaw* inventions, and not necessarily supplied by the railway.

From time to time, Bradshaw dropped a howler, but this could hardly be otherwise with the immense amount of work involved. One of the best was in July 1936, when they attached a 'Buffer' Car to the 10.45 a.m. from Paddington, in order, it was said, to protect it from the 10.55 Torquay train running into it! An early error was due, no doubt, to careless revision. In August 1859, the Scottish North Eastern, which entered Perth from the north-east, refused to pay the charge for the approach to Perth station, for which the Scottish Central, entering from the south-west, had obtained powers. In the row that followed the Scottish North Eastern put up their own temporary Perth terminal station about 300 yards away and called it Glasgow Road. The dispute lasted three months, after which the Scottish North Eastern reverted to using the main station. But *Bradshaw* left Glasgow Road station in the timetable for at least ten years.

The original price of *Bradshaw* was sixpence, a large sum in the early days. By economising in space and good advertising it somehow held this price until January 1916, when it became one shilling. Gradual price rises during the Second World War brought it

A page from the earliest Bradshaw (enlarged).

LONDON TO BIRMINGHAM.

Distance from London.	STATIONS.	Mixed. 6 a.m.	* Mixed Class 8 a.m.	* First calling at M. Stns. 8¾ a.m.	* Mail. 9½ a.m.	Mixed Class. 11 a.m.	* Mixed calling at 1st.cl. Stns. 1 p.m.	Mixed Class. 2 p.m.	* Mixed Short. 5 p.m.	First Class. 6 p.m.	* Mail, Mixed. 8½ p.m.	FARES. 4 in. car. by day pr 1 class 6 in. by night	1st class carriage, 6 inside, by day	2nd class carriage, closed, by night	2nd class carriage, open, by day
Miles		H. M.	H. M.	H. M.	H. M.	H. M.	H. M.	H. M.	H. M.	H. M.	H. M.	S. D.	S. D.	S. D.	S. D.
	LONDON	6 0	8 0	8 45	9 30	11 0	1 0	2 0	5 0	6 0	8 30				
11¼	Harrow	..	8 30	..	..	..	..	2 30	..	6 30	..	3 6	3 0	2 6	2 0
17¾	WATFORD	6 45	8 50	..	..	11 45	1 45	2 50	5 45	6 50	..	5 0	4 6	4 0	3 0
24½	Boxmoor	..	9 10	..	..	..	..	3 10	..	7 10	..	7 0	6 6	5 6	4 [illegible]
28	B. Hampstead	..	9 20	10 5	..	..	..	3 20	..	7 20	..	8 0	7 6	6 6	5 0
31½	TRING	7 25	9 35	..	10 48	12 25	2 25	3 35	6 25	7 37	9 56	9 6	8 6	7 0	5 6
41	Leighton	7 50	10 0	..	..	12 50	2 50	4 0	6 50	8 0	..	12 0	11 0	9 0	7 6
	Bletchley	..	10 15	..	..	..	..	4 15	..	8 15	..	12 6	12 6	10 6	8 6
52½	WOLVERTON	8 15	10 30	11 0	11 41	1 16	3 15	4 30	7 15	8 30	10 54	15 6	14 0	11 6	9 6
60	Roade	..	10 55	..	..	..	..	4 55	7 40	..	..	17 6	16 0	13 6	10 6
63¼	BLISWORTH	8 50	11 5	..	..	1 30	3 50	5 5	7 50	..	..	18 6	17 0	14 0	11 6
69¾	Weedon	9 5	11 25	11 50	12 33	2 5	4 5	5 25	8 5	..	11 50	20 6	18 6	15 6	12 6
75¾	Crick	..	11 45	..	..	..	..	5 45	..	..	..	22 0	20 0	17 0	13 6
83¼	RUGBY	9 40	12 5	.	..	2 40	4 40	6 5	8 40	..	..	24 6	22 6	18 6	15 0
89¼	Brandon	..	12 20	..	..	..	..	6 20	..	..	..	26 0	24 0	20 0	16 0
94	COVENTRY	10 10	12 35	12 50	1 26	3 10	5 10	6 35	9 10	..	1 0	27 6	25 0	21 0	16 6
100¾	Hampton	10 35	1 0	1 15	..	..	..	7 0	..	..	..	29 6	27 0	22 6	18 0
112¼	BIRMINGHAM	11 30	2 0	2 15	2 30	4 30	6 30	3 0	10 30	..	2 0	32 6	30 0	25 0	20 0

There is a Mixed Train from Aylesbury to London at 11 a.m., and one from London to Aylesbury at 3 p.m.

SUNDAY TRAINS.—Times of Departure, Mixed 8 a.m, Mail* 9½ a.m, Mixed to Wolverton 5 p m, Mail,* mixed 8½ p.m.

Children under Ten Years of age, Half-price. Infants in arms, unable to walk, free of charge—Soldiers *en route* are charged under a special agreement.—Dogs are charged for any distance not exceeding 30 miles, 1s.; 65 miles, 2s.; 85 miles 3s.; and the whole distance, 4s. No dogs allowed to be taken inside the Carriages.

Carriages and Horses should be at the Stations a quarter of an hour before the time of departure, and they cannot be forwarded by any train unless there, at the least, five minutes before its time of departure, which time is punctually observed, and after the doors are closed no Passengers can be admitted

To guard against accident and delay, it is especially requested that Passengers will not leave their seats at any of the Stations, except Wolverton (half way), where ten minutes are allowed for refreshment.

A Passenger may claim the seat corresponding to the number on his Ticket, and when not numbered he may take any seat not previously occupied.—No Gratuity, under any circumstances, is allowed to be taken by any Servant of the Company.

Ten minutes are allowed at the Wolverton Central Station, where a female is in attendance, where refreshments may be obtained.

The Trains marked with an asterisk (*) are in conjunction with those of the Grand Junction Railway; sufficient time being allowed at the Birmingham Station, where refreshments are provided, and waiting rooms, with female attendants.

A page from the Intelligible Railway Guide *of June, 1858. Jeoffry Spence Collection.*

to 7s. 6d. Ten shillings was demanded for the issue of 13 June 1955 and the size was increased from very slightly larger than the original 6in by 4¾in to 9in by 6in, the summer issue weighing 3¼ lbs. The tables had all been re-cast and were so tidy and efficient that the publication lost its soul and died in May 1961. It was mourned at any rate by the older generations, who had spent loving hours delving into its endearing idiosyncracies.

Bradshaw's main rival was the *ABC* or 'Alphabetical Railway Guide'. This publication was started in October 1853 and showed 'at a glance how and when to go from London to the principal stations in Great Britain, and return; together with the fares, distances and population'. Anyone in a hurry, and unable to pick their way through the intricacies of *Bradshaw* could, if going to a Principal Station, find it 'as easy as ABC'. To go to Aberdeen, for example, in 1893, the *ABC* gave you the choice of three routes for the first train of the day, all leaving London at 5.15 a.m.: by the Great Northern from King's Cross arriving Aberdeen 8.40 p.m.; by the London & North Western from Euston arriving 9.5 p.m.; and by the Midland arriving at 8.40 p.m. *Bradshaw* did not make it quite so plain. One looked for Aberdeen in the index to be told bluntly that 'From London' it was on pages 244, 328 or 202, which referred to the London & North

Western, Midland and Great Northern respectively, and which was presumably *Bradshaw's* idea of priority of service. But to go to a small station like Abbots Ripton, which from King's Cross was 68¼ miles (63½ in *Bradshaw*, which was more like it) the only information, apart from fares was about 'Departures *from* London as for Holme'.

The *ABC* showed up the paucity of services to some places at a glance. Of later years this tendency became even worse. To take a random example, the service to Blankney & Metheringham (Lincs.) in 1959 consisted of a 4 a.m. from London via Spalding or the 1.18 p.m. on Saturdays. Except for Saturdays, one left London at 2.10 and had to travel via Grantham at a higher fare; a bleak outlook for the bold spirits of Blankney or, indeed, of Metheringham.

In March 1927 the *ABC* started printing arrival and departure times in a new and bolder type-face. Fuller details of train services were now given and double-barrelled station names were cross-referenced. The *ABC*'s only significant rival seems to have been the *A to Z*, the first issue of which was published in May 1935. This included sections on different coloured paper for other forms of transport like Green Line buses. It can never have been a profitable enterprise, for it ceased publication within two years.

Another guide which, like the *ABC*, started life in the 1850s was the *Intelligible Railway Guide*, published by W. Kent & Co., of Paternoster Row, London. It was 'entered at Stationers' Hall, January 29, 1858', the first issue being dated June 1858 but appears only to have lasted until January 1859. A pasted-in slip remarks that

'It is perhaps too much to hope that at the beginning of a work like this *no* mistakes should occur. Few can estimate the magnitude of the task here undertaken in reducing such a mass of facts and figures into a new order, by means of a new staff, and then having the whole to revise with the Official Time-Tables within the shortest possible period just before publication...'

One can well imagine the difficulties. The railway companies were still uncooperative, even with *Bradshaw*, which had now become a household word, and it must have been a nightmare trying to get everything ready in time. It was not until 1902 that the railway companies agreed to send advance notices to *Bradshaw*, and possibly others, to enable the next issue to be ready a week before the first day of the month of operation.

The *Intelligible Guide* had some very good points, and one wonders why it lasted so short a time. It measured about 7½in by 4¾in, with a rather odd collection of engravings on the front cover. The bottom centre was taken up by a large egg-timer, surrounded by a crowd of exhausted-looking passengers with piles of luggage, babies etc., and a uniformed official ringing a station handbell for an approaching unidentifiable engine with what looked like a train of open carriages on a miniature railway. The centre-piece was a large fob watch, and for some curious reason it had large spiders' webs on either side of it. There were clear hints to travellers on how to send luggage: small packages 'that will go conveniently beneath the carriage-seat, should be kept under your own charge and not entrusted to the guard, as that officer has plenty of work to do on the road'; on the taking of a ticket; on the carriage (plain, invalid or bed); on incivility, smoking and dogs.

The timetables themselves were far superior in clarity to anything *Bradshaw* produced. Almost everything was in capitals, with the main stations and the heading of each table in bold capitals. The travellers had an 'uninterrupted table of each line, without being confused by the Branches, which are inserted separately at the top, or the bottom, or in adjoining Pages...' There were no page numbers, and to find the train times required, the station index was referred to, and against the station name was a 'Division Number', and as the Division numbers ran consecutively from 1 to 850 it was a simple matter to find the particular table. Map references, too, were shown in the index. The maps were very clear, and were engraved by Lewis Becker's Patent Process, in steel. There was a key, followed by an enlargement of the

environs of London; and seven regional maps, each double page, were inserted at intervals, and included insets of the larger cities. Like all the guides of the period, it was full of advertisements for quack medicines and corsets, with Sparks & Son's 'India-Rubber Urinals for Male and Female Railway Travellers' jostling for space on the same page as T. Sheppard's 'Stilton Cheese in Splendid Condition'.

A similar type of timetable was the *Easifind*, which first made its appearance in June 1927 at a price of two shillings. It was compiled by Lt. Col. W. Mansfield, who maintained it was of a convenient size to put in the greatcoat pocket with one fold. It was for England and Wales only, with through connections to Scotland. The map was claimed as something new. It had certainly been specially drawn, and showed the routes on which Pullman cars ran, which was a novelty. An unusual item was the Tabular Index 'which by means of vertical and horizontal columns and references enabled one to ascertain quickly the table concerned in a cross-country or town-to-town journey'. It was novel enough for the publishers to state that 'Infringement of the Copyright of this Tabular Index whether such infringement be piracy or larceny, will be proceeded against'. Town plans of the larger cities were included, and these showed the locations of the various stations and the quickest route to get from one to the other.

Like the *Intelligible Guide* the *Easifind* specialised in very clear printing of the timetable pages. Times for p.m. were shown with the hour figures in heavy black. On branch lines where there were only a very few trains, the stations column was placed in the centre with up and down trains on either side, which gave something of a Continental flavour. Suburban services were not included but, like the services in Scotland, these were added at a later date. The press opinions, to which a whole page was devoted after its first appearance, were enthusiastic. The *Hull Evening News* said it was a publication a child could understand, and both the *Leeds Mercury* and the *London Star* said, rather scathingly, that it was a timetable a woman could use. The *Glasgow Citizen* was obviously pleased with it: 'You'll see at a glance exactly how to go' it said, 'and the decrease in profanity in this country should be considerable.' For all that, it must be deemed a failure, and it finished publication in March 1928. It did some good, however, for in 1928 *Bradshaw* was to introduce map references in its station index, although this practice was dropped in 1933.

Cook's Continental Timetable appeared in March 1873 and was at first published quarterly, and monthly from January 1883. The first issue consisted of 140 pages and cost 1s., and was published as the *Cheap*,

EUSTON TO ABERDEEN,

AUGUST 22nd, 1895.

PARTICULARS OF RUNNING BETWEEN

EUSTON AND CARLISLE.

TIMING STATIONS.	Time of passing.	Time between Stations.	Distance between Stations.	Speed in miles per hour.	Average Speed between stops.
	H. M. S.	MINS. SECS.	MILES.		
Euston ... dep.	8 0 0	17 0	17·3	61·0	
Watford ... pass	8 17 0	13 30	14·2	63·1	
Tring ... ,,	8 30 30	12 30	15·0	72·0	
Bletchley ... ,,	8 43 0	34 0	36·0	63·5	Driver, R. Walker.
Rugby ... ,,	9 17 0	13 30	14·6	64·9	64·3 miles per hour.
Nuneaton ... ,,	9 30 30	11 0	13·0	70·9	
Tamworth ... ,,	9 41 30	22 30	23·4	62·4	
Stafford ... ,,	10 4 0	23 30	24·6	62·8	
Crewe... ... arr.	10 27 30				Load, 3=4½
,, ... dep.	10 29 30	21 55	24·1	66·0	
Warrington pass	10 51 25	10 10	11·5	67·9	
Wigan ... ,	11 1 35	13 40	15·5	68·0	
Preston ... ,,	11 15 15	18 50	20·6	65·7	Driver, B. Robinson.
Lancaster ... ,,	11 34 5	5 37	6·5	69·6	67·2 miles per hour.
Carnforth ... ,,	11 39 42	11 28	12·8	67·0	
Oxenholme ... ,,	11 51 10	12 50	13·1	61·2	
Tebay... ... ,,	12 4 0	6 0	5·8	58·0	
Shap Summit ,,	12 10 0	11 0	13·3	72·5	
Penrith ... ,,	12 21 0	14 30	18·0	74·4	
Carlisle ... arr.	12 35 30		299·25		

7 ft. Compound Passenger Engine "Adriatic" from London to Crewe.
6 ft. 6 in. four wheels coupled Passenger Engine "Hardwicke," Crewe to Carlisle.

Timetable applying to the second spate of railway races between London and Scotland, 1895.

Concise and Simple Guide to All the Principal Lines of Railway, Steamers and Diligences on the Continent of Europe 'with a view of supplying a long-felt and oft-expressed want of the Travelling Public'. The cover, then as now, was orange. The guide was originally suggested by John Bredall, an employee of Thomas Cook's who later became company secretary. Even in its early days it was more comprehensive than *Bradshaw*'s *Continental Guide* (first published 1847) which tried to get in too much. In December 1919 they adopted the 24-hour system, being the first British publication to do so, and increased the price to 2s. 6d. Publication was suspended during the Second World War and was resumed in November 1946, with a larger format, an excellent layout, and double the price. *Cook*'s has always been a sound and reliable publication, and used by armchair specialists almost as much as by the travelling public, where a journey to Vladivostok or Peking could be worked out as easily as that to Rome or Madrid. Interesting information, such as Named Express Trains is given. There are maps of rail systems in various countries and of city stations,

8.0 P.M. EXPRESS,

EUSTON TO ABERDEEN,

AUGUST 22nd, 1895.

PARTICULARS OF RUNNING BETWEEN

CARLISLE AND ABERDEEN.

TIMING STATIONS.	Time of Passing.	Time between Stations.	Distance between Stations.	Speed in Miles per hour.	Average speed between stops.
	H. M. S.	MINS. SECS.	MILES.		
Carlisle ... dep.	12 38 0	39 30	39·75	60·3	
Beattock ... pass	1 17 30	13 30	10· 0	44·4	
,, Summit ,,	1 31 0	21 0	23·75	67·8	Driver, A. Crooks, Engine No. 90.
Carstairs ... ,,	1 52 0	10 30	10· 5	60·0	
Law Junction ,,	2 2 30	5 0	5·75	69·0	60·5 miles per hour.
Holytown ... ,,	2 7 30	19 30	20· 0	61·5	
Larbert ... ,,	2 27 0	7 30	8· 0	64·0	
Stirling ... ,,	2 34 30	33 0	33· 0	60·0	
Perth ... ... arr.	3 7 30				Load 3=4½
,, ... dep.	3 9 30	29 30	32· 5	66·1	
Forfar... ... pass	3 39 0	18 0	19·25	64·2	Driver, J. Souttar, Engine No. 17.
Kinnaber Jun. ,,	3 57 0	12 30	15· 5	74·4	
Drumlithie... ,,	4 9 30	7 0	6·75	57·8	65·4 miles per hour.
Stonehaven ,,	4 16 30				
Aberdeen—					
Ticket Statn. arr	4 30 0	15 30	16· 0	61·9	
,, ,, dep.	4 31 0				
Aberdeen ... arr	4 32 0		240·75		

6 ft. 6 in. four wheels coupled Passenger Engines.

with the distance between those stations stated – even for those that 'adjoined'.

All railway companies, large and small, had their own timetables, and some of them, like the Great Central, were very colourful in their cover design. Almost all had good, large maps suggesting that the through routes to distant parts of the kingdom were all part of their small system. Each company had its own Service, or Working, Timetable. This was for the use of company's servants only and was not for publication. Working timetables gave more detailed information, including passing times at certain points, movements of goods trains, empty stock and light engines. At one time they provided such interesting information as that for example, the early Sunday morning train from Brighton to London Bridge which 'Stops Balcombe Tunnel signal box to set down can of water', and was allowed two minutes less waiting time at Three Bridges to make up for it. Times at stations did not necessarily agree with those shown in the public book, in which a departure would often be earlier in order to get straggling or recalcitrant passengers on to the train in good time. These working timetables, although private, are collectors' items, and are to be found in the homes of most railway enthusiasts.

Highland poster timetable of 1905.

Station Lamps and Other Accessories

Gordon Biddle

Stations built in the first twenty or thirty years of railways in Britain were notable for the quality of their varied architectural styles, generally of a homely domestic character enlivened here and there by richer stuff, and punctuated by the imposing grandeur of the big city termini. As the railways spread and their owning companies grew, the standardisation of structures and fixtures developed with them so that by the 1880s the stamp of a company's ownership was as apparent in many of its stations as in the colour and styling of its locomotives and carriages. Conversely, some of the more durable of early fittings were so long-lived that by the 20th century, mixed with later additions, they presented an enormous variety. Platform lamps in particular, despite adaptations, escaped large-scale replacement until very recent times, so that seven or eight years ago one could still see a fascinating mixture by visiting just a few stations in one locality.

Large stations were lit by gas from the beginning. Contemporary illustrations of stations in the 1830s and 1840s often show small iron lanterns in clusters of two or three on graceful brackets fitted to walls and roof columns, but thereafter various patterns of glass globe appear. Euston had small globes on scrolled brackets over the platforms and on short, elegant columns around the Great Hall balcony; at Bristol Temple Meads, globes hung from the roof on long lengths of piping. By the mid-century, iron baskets were being introduced, suspended over the platforms to contain gas globes, as at Metropolitan stations in London such as Baker Street and Kensington High Street, and the London, Chatham & Dover's station at Victoria; or they might be supported on decorative iron standards like the cruciform pattern at Charing Cross on the South Eastern Railway. Later still, globes gave way to cylindrical glass lanterns, curved at the base. At York and Darlington Bank Top on the North Eastern Railway they fitted into elaborately moulded iron collars, but plain on the London & North Western at Carnforth and Penrith, while the Furness Railway chose a hexagonal framed type at Whitehaven Bransty.

Small country stations, where lighting was usually by oil, provided the greatest variety in attractively shaped lanterns and decorative iron posts. Street lighting patterns were followed, but with shorter posts in scale with station buildings. Lanterns nearly always were square in section and of two principal types: a removable one in an iron cage or frame from which it could be lifted for cleaning, or a fixed lantern on four short, curved stems fixed to an iron collar on top of the post. The glass sides invariably tapered outwards from the base and one side was hinged so that the lamp could be taken out for cleaning, trimming and filling—a daily task for which a special lamp room would be provided on the platform.

Gas lanterns were similar, and indeed as gas distribution extended were often converted from oil lanterns. The South Eastern had a number of sharply tapered square lanterns which imparted a degree of elegance, while the London & North Western later standardised on a distinctive hexagonal gas lantern

An array of GWR gas lamps at Tilehurst. The three nearest the camera still carry their wartime blackout hoods.

so narrow at the base that it almost formed an inverted pyramid. The tops were usually iron, but sometimes white or plain glass, in which the Great Northern had an attractive curved design, and surmounted by a decorative ventilator which again displayed a wide amount of variation. The North Eastern, for instance, had a plain circular ventilator, perforated like a pepper pot; the London & South Western ventilator was butterfly shaped; the Midland Railway favoured three frilly tiers tipped by a spike; and the Midland & Great Northern Joint line had some bell-shaped designs. Oddities abounded, like the 'arch' sided lanterns at Manorbier on the Great Western, with square front and curved metal top, probably dating from the original Pembroke & Tenby Railway. A memorable Great Western design, now almost disappeared, comprised a tapered lantern suspended in a large vertical hoop of irregular shape, rather squashed in appearance and embellished with scrolls.

Short wooden posts were cheaper than iron. They were common at oil-lit stations on the North Eastern where the lantern sat in a plain, square, horizontal hoop projecting from the top. Hull & Barnsley Railway station lamps were similar and after 1923 when those companies became part of the London & North Eastern Railway, the wooden posts as they wore out were replaced by concrete. The London & North Western

company, too, adopted a very utilitarian oil lantern in its later years, square with a backward-sloping top and glazed on three sides, the metal back having a slot to fit over a locomotive-type lamp iron fixed to a convenient wall, fence or short wooden post. These also were perpetuated after the grouping by the London, Midland and Scottish.

But generally, oil and gas lanterns were on cast iron posts or standards with a crossbar near the top against which a ladder could be set. The early ones were often cast by local foundries, like Harwell & Co of Northampton who made some of the lamp posts on the Midland between Leicester and Hitchin, or Smith & Sons of Whitchurch. As standard styles became the rule, the local touch was lost; vast numbers of sturdy hexagonal posts made by Handyside of Derby could be seen all over the Midland Railway's system from Cumberland to South Wales, bearing the names of the foundry and the railway and, sometimes, the date of manufacture. The London & South Western and South Eastern companies used twisted spiral posts, like barley-sugar sticks, a design followed somewhat differently by the Great Central Railway for its London Extension where the gas lamps had ornate crossbars shaped like wings. Other companies' posts might be attractively fluted, as in some early London & North Western, Great Eastern and Great Western designs, although later on the North Western and Great Western changed to a hexagonal style like the Midland's. The Lancashire & Yorkshire Railway, always of an austere frame of mind, had a decidedly

Top row, left to right:

North Eastern oil lantern in an iron hoop attached to a concrete post, Arram.

LBSCR decorated iron oil lamp with fixed ladder, Grange Road.

LSWR oil lamp on twisted iron column, Asbury. Note the 'butterfly' style ventilator.

Bottom row, left to right:

North Eastern oil lamp in iron cage on fluted column with initials cast in the crossbar, the ends of which have been removed, Bardon Mill.

Great Central iron lamp post with Sugg Rochester lamp, Brackley.

Standard Midland gas lamp at Aldridge.

plain lamp post, tapering from a curved base and thriftily dependent upon a single bar projecting from one side for the lamp man's ladder. Rather taller, plain posts were erected at Blencow on the Cockermouth, Keswick & Penrith Railway, enlivened by a decorated crossbar. The North Eastern, among a small group of companies, had their initials cast on the crossbar, and occasionally one came across a reminder of some long-defunct company like the Inverness & Ross-shire Railway's name on the posts at Invergordon. Unusual slender iron posts were found at some North Staffordshire Railway stations, with a decorated bracket and hoop for the lantern projecting from the top.

Although they were not common, specially decorated lamp posts were provided when the company felt a gesture was needful, like the series at Wolferton, the Great Eastern's station for Sandringham, where the lanterns bore miniature royal arms on all four sides of the upper rim and a gilded crown on top of the ventilator. Elsewhere the same company was decidedly utilitarian in using lengths of old rail as lamp posts, a practice followed also on the Somerset & Dorset Joint line.

The post-grouping companies gradually replaced the old gas lanterns with the ugly Sugg Rochester lamp, with its broad-brimmed 'top hat' over a semi-circular globe, often fitted to the original post by an even uglier swan-necked pipe. Tall, harsh concrete standards transformed many Southern Railway stations, ubiquitous erections with curved brackets for both gas and electric lighting and, on the Great Western, for oil lamps, too, with a small windlass and pulley for hoisting and lowering.

Among the first stations to be lit by electricity in the 1880s were Charing Cross, Cannon Street, Paddington and the Manchester, Sheffield & Lincolnshire Railway's section of Manchester London Road station (the London & North Western's portion of the station continued to be gas lit for a long time). Lamps were fairly uniform, small white globes being held beneath a large cylindrical fitting suspended from the roof. The LNER kept to the white globe and then tried a shallow rectangular glass shade bearing the station name. Large hexagonal shades were introduced by the Southern as it proceeded to rebuild or modernise many of its suburban stations. The Great Western and the LMSR were the less progressive pair in the 'big four', the latter company even perpetuating gas lighting at some of its new stations.

In these days of compact luggage, drip-dry clothing and lightweight fabrics, pre-war rail travel with large suitcases and trunks seems very remote. In Victorian times, when the middle and upper classes removed entire households to the seaside or country for a month or more each summer, 'travelling light' was unknown

and railway stations had to cope with even more baggage than usual. A good complement of two-wheel barrows was essential for the hand luggage and four-wheel trolleys for the larger items and parcels traffic. Barrows have tended to disappear but many old wooden trolleys are still in use, with iron wheels and a central handle which, when released, springs upright and applies a brake. In former years barrows and trolleys had the station name painted on one side. Between the wars, petrol tractors for pulling trains of barrows were introduced at large stations. Nowadays quieter battery vehicles are used. Mail trolleys usually had wooden rails at each end and some had their wheels arranged in a diamond pattern for easy manoeuvrability. At one time St Pancras was provided with a special trolley for handling coffins.

Another vanishing piece of equipment is the train indicator. On the platforms it usually consisted of one or more clock-faces on a post, the hands of which could be moved round to show the departure time. A series of destination boards was kept on a rack beneath, slots being provided under each clock-face into which the appropriate board fitted. On the concourse a large wooden departure indicator might be seen, with a series of slats which could be adjusted to show the correct sequence of stations at which trains called. Some are still in use, and the roller blind type of indicator is still very familiar although, with the adoption of departure sheets instead of timetables for public display, they are now tending to disappear.

Timetable boards are a thing of the past, nowadays being used for showing departure sheets and advertisements instead of the array of timetables covering both local lines and a good many more distant ones as well. In later years, they were enlarged reprints from the timetable book, and on the Great Western the separate Sunday service tables were heavily overprinted 'Sunday' in red, diagonally across the sheet.

Maps of the system were familiar in carriages, but at least three companies displayed them at stations in glazed, coloured wall tiles. The London, Brighton & South Coast had two at Victoria, one showing main lines and the other suburban routes, both now hidden by hoardings and telephone kiosks. At Manchester Victoria the Lancashire & Yorkshire Railway map is still very prominent, painted in black on white tiles. Tiled wall maps really proliferated on the North Eastern where they were part of the decor at many of the company's principal stations. Mass produced, they were a mine of information, including large-scale insets of the lines at Tyne Dock, Middlesbrough, the Hartlepools and Hull docks, and a selection of sites of battlefields, cathedrals, abbeys, castles and country seats.

Every station of importance, and a good many

Great Eastern oil lantern at Shirebrook North.　　　　LNWR oil lantern at Dolwyddelen.

lesser ones as well, had its complement of automatic vending machines for chocolates, cigarettes and platform tickets. They were not the flimsy sheet metal boxes of today but tall cast iron machines on a tapered stand with an enamel display panel and a large brass handle for pulling out the delivery tray. Heavy iron die-stamping machines which produced embossed letters on aluminium strip, twelve letters for a penny, were also popular, but nowadays those that remain are smaller and produce plastic. Although weighing machines are still with us, albeit consigned to the lavatories, they have disappeared from the small country junctions—themselves now few in number— whereas in former years many stations were incomplete without a large, cumbersome slot machine mounted with a pair of brass handrails.

Large-scale vitreous enamelling processes were perfected in the first part of the 19th century and from the 1850s onwards were widely used for advertisement signs. The railways quickly seized on this means of gaining extra revenue and enamel advertisements appeared on station walls and fences, on occasions in such large numbers that it was difficult to see the wall at all. They lasted a long time and by present-day sophisticated advertising standards doubtless seem prosaic, but at least they were brief and to the point: Virol, Stephens' Ink, Earles Cement, Pears Soap, Epps' Cocoa, and Sutton's Seeds were impressed on the mind at countless stations, while Mazzawattee Tea

ascended before the eyes in blue and yellow on the stair risers of many a station footbridge.

Illustrations of early stations rarely show notice boards. Instructions were given verbally by the staff but, as travel increased and stations grew in complexity, by mid-century no railway establishment was complete without its crop of informative or directional signs. Frequently they were formed of iron letters screwed to a wooden board. Parsimonious or impecunious companies like the South Eastern used painted boards and later some lines adopted vitreous enamel. The London & North Western, the North Eastern and the Hull & Barnsley, for example, used enamel for small door plates, but the Midland and the Great Western favoured hanging enamelled signs as well, although it was left to the London Underground railways to standardise enamelled notices. Etched window glass was used extensively to indicate waiting and refreshment rooms, while frilly-edged cast iron signs were standard on the Great Central's London Extension.

The most fascinating thing about station signs was their terminology. It varied according to the company's attitude towards its passengers. No great concern was shown about the niceties of grammar, and large letters were used to give emphasis in a most haphazard fashion, with curious results. Stations had no exits, only a 'Way Out'—which was clear enough—or, just in case there might be lingering doubts at Admaston on the GW and LNW Joint line in Shropshire, 'The Way Out'. Crossing the line was severely regulated according to whether there was a bridge, subway or foot crossing.

Station nameboards were particularly important. At some of the very early stations the name was inscribed on a stone panel–the Chester & Holyhead Railway had them in slate–but generally large wooden boards were placed at the platform ends, later supplemented by small etched glass panels in platform lamps which illuminated them at night, and in the London area on the Great Northern and the London, Brighton & South Coast Railways, in station building windows. For their main boards, most railways used bold cast iron letters screwed on, surrounded by a moulded edge and mounted on two posts, to which the Midland and the London & South Western added small decorative brackets. As became a railway based on the Potteries, the North Staffordshire's earlier nameboards were composed of individual glazed earthenware lettered tiles, probably by Minton (Colin Minton Campbell was chairman of the board from 1874 to 1883). The very large boards suspended from the roofs at Crewe and Rugby, displaying the name in gigantic sans-serif letters, for long were familiar features. Some of the early London & North Western nameboards had had pleasantly chubby seriffed lettering like the one behind the buffer stops at Banbury, where it remained long after closure in 1961.

Frequently, junction station nameboards carried a reminder to passengers to change trains, although a knowledge of railway geography was sometimes needful. The terse 'Junction for the Severn Valley Line' which appeared beneath 'Hartlebury' on the Great Western was unusual for that company, which more often noted a wealth of connecting services on boards frequently so large that they needed an extra post in the middle. At times the catalogue of stations for which one should change was more a public relations exercise than of practical value.

Post-grouping standardisation was applied equally to nameboards, except on the Great Western which perpetuated its former style, and in the 1930s new ideas spread through the LMS and the Southern Railway in particular. On the LMS large-scale replacement of pre-grouping nameboards took place, in favour of a cast light alloy plate with a central circular motif, fixed to a sheet metal back in a wooden frame. Painted yellow with black lettering and lining, they were much smaller and neater than the older boards but less easily read from a passing train. Small matching enamel plates were hung beneath the platform lamps.

The Southern produced a dark green enamelled plate with white lettering which in many instances was fitted to an old board from which the iron letters

GWR platform ticket machine.

had been removed. Lamp nameplates took the form of a bar-and-circle motif, not unlike that adopted on the Underground but on a shaped plate. The Great Western's only concession was to fit small black-and-white enamelled plates to platform lamps, similar to ones introduced by the LNER.

Station platforms accommodated a host of other miscellaneous items, such as portable wooden steps at old stations having low platforms, and dated drinking

Lancashire & Yorkshire wooden departure indicator, Manchester Victoria.

Cheshire Lines Committee drinking fountain at Widney North, dated 1872.

fountains at some Midland and Cheshire Lines stations. No station was complete without its array of fire buckets, boldly lettered. Platform benches, despite enormous variety, generally were of proprietary makes on many lines where several different patterns could be seen, usually of the public park or seaside promenade type. A number of companies, however, used the spaces between the cast iron legs at each end to display their monogrammed initials or emblem, such as the London, Tilbury & Southend, the Great Eastern and the Great Western, the latter's curly lettered monogram being superseded after grouping by solid cast leg-ends bearing the company's well-known circular motif devised for publicity purposes. 'CR Co' appeared in the ends of Cambrian Railways seats, and on the Furness Railway a most elaborate design included what has been called its squirrel-and-nuts emblem, although the animal looks somewhat hybrid. It has been suggested that it was really intended to represent 'the little foxes that spoil the vines' from the Song of Solomon. At all events, with the lavish foliage and hawks-head armrest it forms a fine period piece.

The Midland and the Great Central tended to concentrate on a pseudo-rustic bench with knobbly legs and armrests, but otherwise without decoration, whereas many companies used the backrest to display the station name in cast iron letters, usually recessed but sometimes with individual letters screwed straight on – a particularly uncomfortable method.

Inside the station waiting rooms wooden benches offered varying degrees of comfort, from the bare form fitted to the wall at some of the oldest and more primitive stations to the black leatherette and horsehair upholstery provided at the more important places. Company initials could be seen carved on the backrests: a gothic letter 'M' on the dark polished wood of Midland seats; 'S&MJL', for Sheffield and Midland Joint Line, at Marple and New Mills Central; 'MB&M' (for Macclesfield, Bollington & Marple) as reminders of the original owner of the Great Central & North Staffordshire Joint line. In the waiting rooms at Knott Mill (now Deansgate) on the Manchester South Junction & Altrincham Railway (L&NW and Great Central Joint) the painted letters 'MSJ' – by which the

Pigeon baskets, trolleys and portable water tanks for replenishing dining car tanks, Leicester Central, GCR.

line was popularly known—were considered sufficient indication of ownership, although the Great Central itself went to the other extreme of having inlaid brass letters on its station dining room chairs.

No waiting room was complete without a large polished table in the centre, while the fireplace or iron stove afforded yet more scope for advertising the company. Initials were frequently cast or carved on curbs and mantelpieces, the Great Northern using a monogrammed shield at Peakirk, for instance, while the North Staffordshire's knot emblem appeared on every stove door. The last word—or words—go to the Latin inscriptions on the huge stone Tudoresque fireplaces in the refreshment room at Carlisle.

Not only was royalty favoured with private waiting rooms, as at the two Windsor stations and Wolferton, but, where patronage or expediency demanded, the nobility as well. Berkhamsted was rebuilt by the London & North Western in 1875 with 'a permanent suite of rooms, with octagonal hall and external verandah', according to *The Builder*, for the use of Earl Brownlow, and appropriately furnished. Redmile, the

station for Belvoir, bore the Duke of Rutland's arms on the external brickwork and a carved depiction of his castle, with the Belvoir hunt in full cry in the foreground, over the huge ornate wooden fireplace in his private waiting room, together with armchairs, table, and carpets. At Rowsley, the station for Chatsworth, however, the Duke of Devonshire's guests had to share the 'Gentlemen's Room First Class', which as recently as 1962 was fully furnished with two leather sofas, an armchair—inscribed with the Midland Railway's inevitable 'M'—and an assortment of travelling rugs.

First class waiting rooms had better furnishings than second and third, of course, with such luxuries as umbrella stands and carpets. There was a long-standing oddity at Garsdale station, on the Midland's Settle and Carlisle line remote in the northern Pennines, where the waiting room contained a harmonium and a bookcase for the occasions when it served the scattered local community as chapel and library.

Just as the old dining rooms have been replaced by quick-service cafeterias, so the old waiting rooms have virtually disappeared, though original seating may be found in some country stations. What remains is usually on the platform itself and of an appropriately desirable nature.

This page, top to bottom:
Great Eastern decorated iron knifeboard seat with the company's coat of arms, Huntingdon East.
Taff Vale wooden platform seats, Pontypridd.
Furness Railway cast iron seat end at Grange-over-Sands.

Opposite page:
Honeybourne Junction Station, GWR, now partly demolished. This was the interchange point on the Worcester to Paddington line for Stratford-upon-Avon and Cheltenham. Note the typical junction station nameboard.
A group of shunting horns and whistles from New Street Station, Birmingham. Cattell Collection.

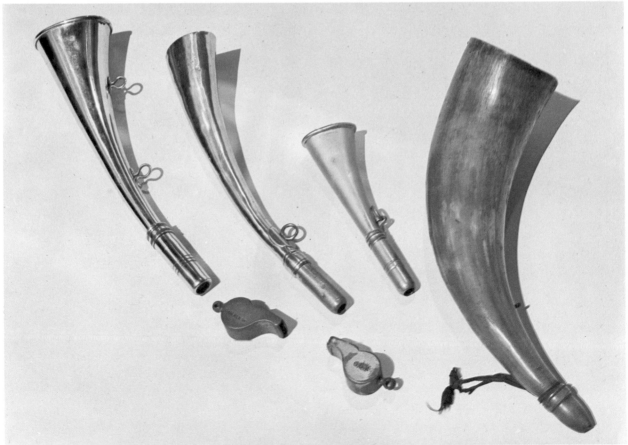

An NER trespass notice from South Church, Bishop Auckland. This was where the Stockton & Darlington Railway built a platform in May 1842 which enabled them to offer a through service to Rainton Meadows by horse bus until November 1843, so turning the east-west railway into part of the north-south route.

Cast Iron and Enamel Signs and Notices

Graham Thomas

Public notices in one form or another have been part of the railway scene almost as long as the railways themselves. However it was not until the middle of the 19th century that the familiar cast iron and enamel signs began to appear. No one can be certain when the first sign went up, but possibly the earliest is a Midland Railway notice erected in about 1845, for it bears the name J. F. Bell, who was secretary to the company from 1844 to 1853.

From the mid-century onwards, signs of many kinds, displaying all sorts of information were put up by the railway companies, at track sides, at stations and crossings, on buildings and bridges, by railway-owned canals, and sometimes even on rolling stock. Not all the notices so displayed were intended for the general public; many were in places where they could only have been seen by railway company servants, but such examples are worthy of inclusion, because of their great variety and for the interesting information which they provide.

Broadly speaking, public notices can be divided into four categories: trespass notices; warning notices (including bridge restriction signs); road, footpath and towpath notices; and company's servants notices. Bridge number plates and boundary posts are also included here since they are usually collected along with cast iron and enamel signs.

Trespass signs are the largest and possibly the most important group of public notices, and vast numbers of them were erected by the bigger railway companies. The LNWR and the L&Y, for example, made a habit of putting them up virtually at every point where the public was likely to come into contact with railway-owned land and might consequently be tempted to trespass. Familiar locations are the end of station platforms, level crossings, and at the foot of an embankment. A typical level crossing would have a trespass notice displayed on each side of the track, suitably placed so that it could be read by the public. Occasionally a warning notice would be fixed below, but this practice was more typical of unstaffed crossings such as those used by farmers, and at footpath crossings.

It is at the unstaffed crossings that some companies really excelled themselves. A typical example in Wales might have no less than six notices displayed. Four would be of the trespass type, two in English and two in Welsh, while the remaining two would be 'Gate' notices. The English language ones are of the standard LNWR 'Caution' type found all over the company's system, but the Welsh ones are peculiar to lines in Wales, for although they are similarly worded they have no company name at the top. They were thus never used singly, but always in association with the English version. This double form of trespass notice is unique, though the Great Western and the Rhymney railways produced some bilingual ones.

The LNWR did not neglect unstaffed crossings in England either, for in place of the Welsh notice the company usually put a warning sign. Many other companies treated such crossings in the same way. The Great Western often provided two gate and two trespass notices on each occasion and two trespass notices at a footpath crossing. Strangely enough, other companies ignored the farming community between whose fields the lines passed, providing them with no notices whatsoever. This had nothing to do with the financial standing of the company, for the Stratford-upon-Avon & Midland Junction Railway, hardly a prosperous line, saw fit to erect two trespass notices at every farmers' and footpath crossing. On the other hand the North Staffordshire Railway, one of the better off small pre-grouping companies, never put up trespass notices at farmers' crossings, although they did when footpaths crossed their lines.

The general layout of a trespass notice did not vary greatly from company to company, and the LNWR 'Caution' may be taken as standard. First comes the warning of the danger of trespassing on company lands, then a reference to the relevant Act which forbids it and finally the penalties imposed for the offence, if committed. In addition to this rather elaborate form of notice many railways produced a smaller and more succinct version, usually with 'Trespassers will be Prosecuted' in large letters across the centre. This, together with the company's name at the top and often 'By Order' on the lower right-hand side was considered sufficient to deter the would-be trespasser. There seems to be no logical reason for this duplication, for both types of notice can be found in similar locations being used to the same effect. Larger companies producing both types include the Midland, the Great Western, London and South Western and Great Northern railways.

It is a curious fact that while most English and Welsh railways produced trespass notices in great numbers, they are scarce in Scotland. Only the North British and Highland railways made them in cast iron and enamel; the Caledonian, Great North of Scotland and the Dundee & Arbroath used only enamel ones, and these in small quantities. Enamel is far less durable than cast iron and suffers badly from exposure. Consequently Scottish company notices, even in a poor condition, are highly prized collectors' items.

Interesting variations of the standard trespass notice are those found on joint lines and joint stations. The remarks which follow apply also to warning, road, footpath and towpath notices and to company's servants signs where these exist on joint railways. Three types of notice from joint lines can be distinguished. The first type bears an amalgamation of the names of the owning companies, eg Great Central & Midland Joint Line. In this case the signs were usually cast by one or sometimes both of the companies, and are thus variations of the pattern used on their own lines. There was no hard and fast rule stating which of the owning companies should cast

the notices for a particular joint line. The LNWR, for example, the Midland's partner in the rather unholy alliance of the Midland & LNW Joint, cast them for this line and, as is to be expected, they are variations of the LNW 'Caution'. Yet, oddly enough, the Midland provided the boundary posts for this line. A similar state of affairs exists on the GN&LNW Joint, the LNWR casting the notices and the GNR providing the boundary posts. The second category of joint notices are those which were cast by one of the parent companies although the joint line had its own individual title, eg the Somerset & Dorset Joint Line owned by the London & South Western and Midland Railways. The S&DJR trespass notice is a standard LSWR casting with alterations in the appropriate places to suit the joint line. There were, however, some joint lines in existence whose notices fall into both of the above groups. For example, the Methley Joint Railway, owned by the Great Northern, North Eastern and Lancashire & Yorkshire railways, had signs cast by the GNR with either the initials of the owning companies at the top, or, alternatively, Methley Joint Railway. Similarly the West Riding & Grimsby Railway has notices bearing this title or GN&GC Joint; again they are GNR in origin. The third group of notices are those from a joint line with its own title and distinctive signs. The Cheshire Lines Committee is a good example, its notices being unlike those of the GCR, Midland or GNR. Finally it should be mentioned that standard notices belonging to one or both of the owning companies are often found alongside the specially cast joint version on joint lines.

Prior to 1923, there were about twenty-five joint stations, but notices from these are rare. Carlisle Citadel was provided with a specially cast notice and so was Stalybridge Joint Station.

Warning notices were never erected by the railways in the same numbers as trespass signs. Furthermore, the information they display tends on the whole to be simpler, for the intention is to warn of impending danger which is more likely to be imminent at unstaffed crossings, and the lettering is therefore bolder. (Exceptions include some bridge restriction notices, which often have long and complex wording, and the occasional gate notice.)

Typical warning notices are those that tell the public to 'Beware of Trains' and many railways provided signs with this message in large letters. More informative are those that not only warn people to beware of trains, but also to 'Look both up and down the line before you cross'. Other notices sometimes threaten offenders with prosecution if they attach their own notices to a railway-owned wall or fence. 'Stick no Bills' is usually sufficient to deter, but if not, in stronger terms, 'Bill Stickers will be Prosecuted'.

LONDON AND NORTH WESTERN RAILWAY
CAUTION

PERSONS TRESPASSING UPON THE RAILWAYS BELONGING TO, OR LEASED OR WORKED BY, THE LONDON AND NORTH WESTERN RAILWAY COMPANY, OR BY THAT COMPANY AND ANY OTHER COMPANY, AND ANY PERSONS TRESPASSING UPON THE STATIONS CONNECTED WITH SUCH RAILWAYS, ARE LIABLE TO A PENALTY OF **FORTY SHILLINGS**, UNDER THE LONDON AND NORTH WESTERN RAILWAY ADDITIONAL POWERS ACT, 1883, AND, IN ACCORDANCE WITH THE PROVISIONS OF THE SAID ACT, PUBLIC WARNING IS HEREBY GIVEN TO ALL PERSONS, NOT TO TRESPASS UPON THE SAID RAILWAYS OR STATIONS.

EUSTON STATION LONDON
DECEMBER 1883

BY ORDER

RHYBUDD

MAE PERSONAU DRESPASONT AR REILFFYRDD YN CAEL EU PERCHENOGI NEU EU PRYDLESU GAN GWMPEINI Y LONDON & NORTH WESTERN RAILWAY, NEU YN CAEL EU GWEITHIO GANDDYNT, NEU GANDDYNT HWY AC UNRHYW GWMPEINI ARALL AC HEFYD UNRHYW BERSONAU DRESPASONT AR ORSAFOEDD Y CYFRYW REILFFYRDD YN AGORED I DDIRWY O **DDEUGAIN SWLLT**, O DAN Y LONDON & NORTH WESTERN RAILWAY, ADDITIONAL POWERS ACT, 1883, AC YN UNOL A THELERAU YR ACT DDYWEDEDIG RHODDIR TRWY HYN I BAWB RYBUDD CYHOEDDUS I BEIDIO TRESPASU AR Y RHEILFFYRDD NAC AR Y GORSAFOEDD DYWEDEDIG.

GORSAF EUSTON LLUNDAIN
RHAGFYR, 1883,

TRWY ORCHYMYN.

LNWR trespass notice of 1883 with the Welsh language version beneath it; a unique form of double sign. Winchcombe Railway Museum.

Stratford-upon-Avon & Midland Junction Railway combined trespass and warning notice. It is unusual in providing both of these functions. Graham Thomas Collection.

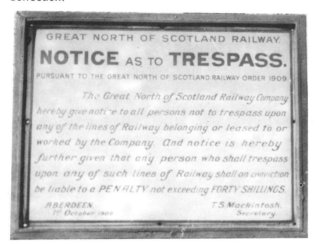

GNSR enamel trespass notice. The wooden frame was commonly used in conjunction with an enamel sign. This example is well preserved—compare with the example from the Halesowen Railway.

LNWR 'simple' type trespass notice. The wooden post is nearly always used with this notice, whereas the caution sign always has an angle iron support, unless fixed to a building or wall.

Gates at unstaffed crossings often have notices attached to them stating that the gates must be 'Shut and Fastened after Use' and occasionally the penalty is added, usually forty shillings. The LNWR went in for something a little more emphatic on their gate notices, for they quoted the relevant Act of Parliament which made it illegal to leave the gate open, and presumably made anyone think very carefully before doing so!

Weighbridges in station yards often provide a reason for a notice, the GWR casting a neat little one for such a purpose. Other notices that can be included here are fire bucket notices, expressing the need to keep fire buckets full of water. The Midland & Great Northern Joint and the Somerset & Dorset Joint both produced rather ornate examples. A great favourite among collectors is the Great Western signal box door notice, which proclaims 'No unauthorized person allowed in this box'. Some, possibly earlier, versions had 'is' inserted between 'person' and 'allowed'.

Last but not least are the bridge restriction notices, often providing both a warning and, at times, some rather indigestible information. They can be simple, like the Shropshire Union Railway & Canal Company example, which warns that the bridge is 'insufficient to carry weights beyond the ordinary traffic of the district', or more specific, as with the Great Eastern notice which refers to 'locomotives and other unusually heavy traffic' as being unsuitable vehicles. A few companies, such as the Cambrian Railways provided detailed information as to the limitations of the bridge. Road, footpath and towpath notices were erected at places owned by a railway company to which the public were allowed conditional access.

Notices erected for the attention of railway company servants can often be both intriguing and informative. The L&Y produced a variety of such signs. An unusual

A very rare Halesowen Railway enamel notice. Although in poor condition, it would be almost priceless today.

GREAT CENTRAL R.Y.
TRESPASSERS ON THIS PROPERTY
WILL BE PROSECUTED.

CHESHIRE LINES COMMITTEE.
NOTICE.
ANY PERSON TRESPASSING ON THIS
RAILWAY WILL BE PROSECUTED.
BY ORDER.

Standard Great Central trespass notice. Winchcombe Railway Museum.

Cheshire Lines Committee trespass notice which should be compared with examples from its owning companies, GCR, Midland and GNR. Winchcombe Railway Museum.

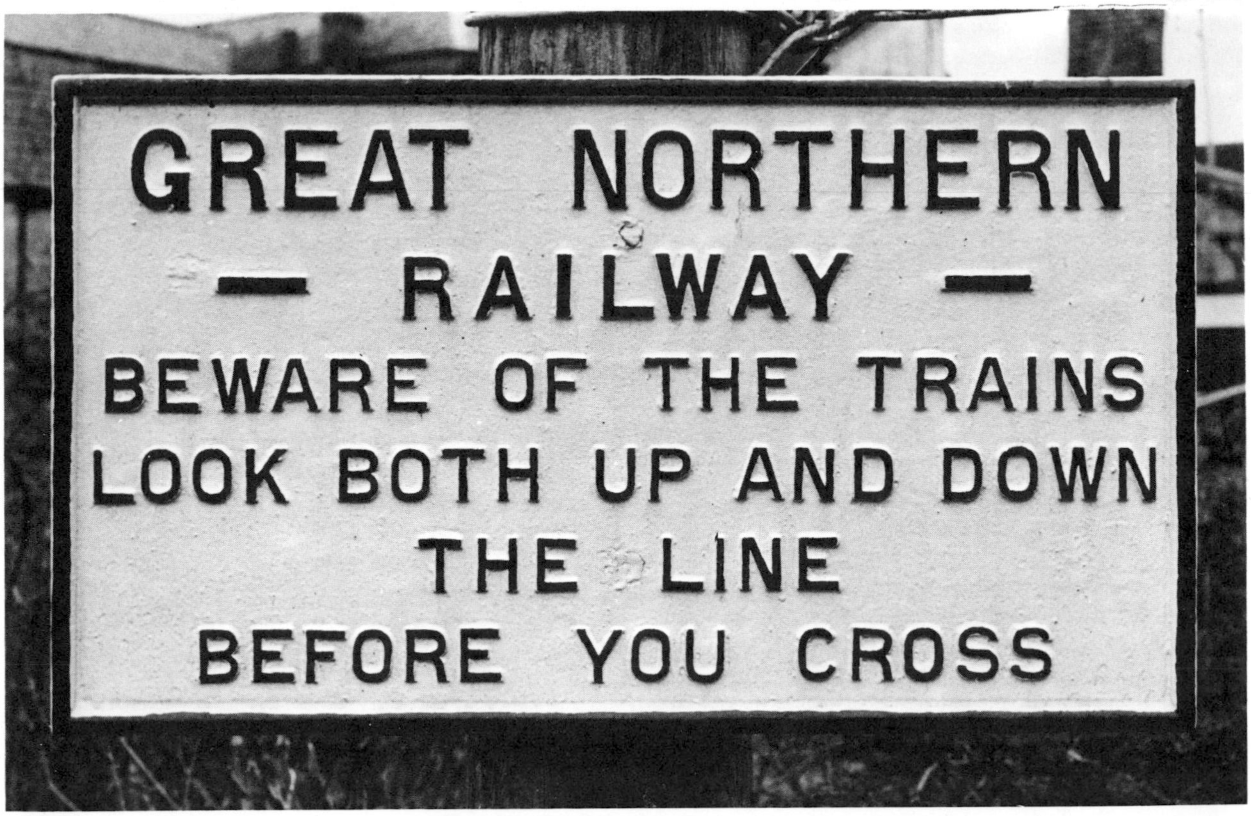

GREAT NORTHERN RAILWAY

— RAILWAY —

BEWARE OF THE TRAINS
LOOK BOTH UP AND DOWN
THE LINE
BEFORE YOU CROSS

GREAT CENTRAL RAILWAY
COMPANY

NOTICE

BILL POSTERS WILL BE PROSECUTED
BY ORDER

Great Northern Railway warning notice with typical wording which many other companies used. Winchcombe Railway Museum.

Great Central Railway 'bill stickers' notice. Note the two different styles of lettering. Winchcombe Railway Museum.

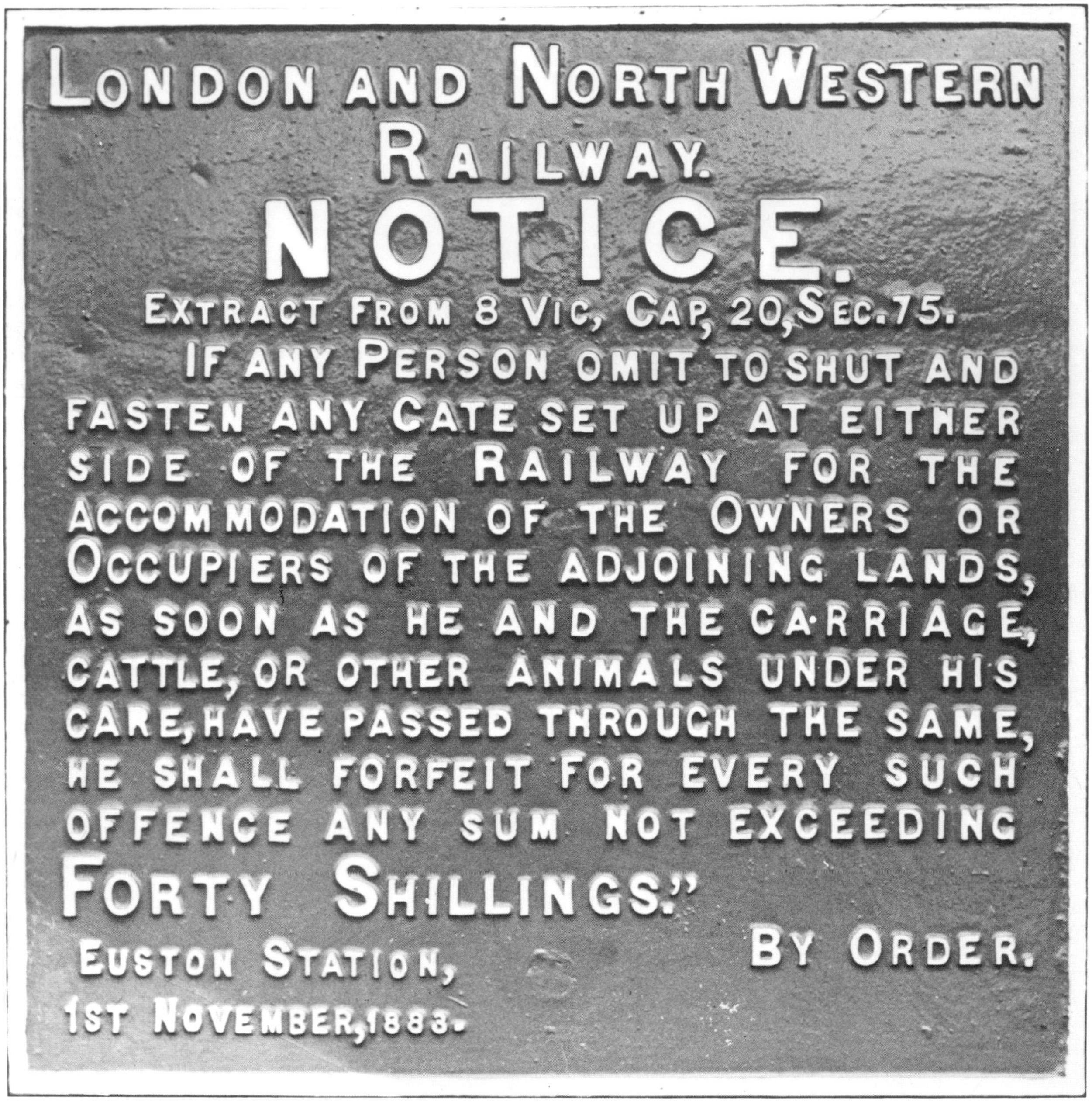

LONDON AND NORTH WESTERN RAILWAY.

NOTICE.

EXTRACT FROM 8 VIC, CAP, 20, SEC. 75.

IF ANY PERSON OMIT TO SHUT AND FASTEN ANY GATE SET UP AT EITHER SIDE OF THE RAILWAY FOR THE ACCOMMODATION OF THE OWNERS OR OCCUPIERS OF THE ADJOINING LANDS, AS SOON AS HE AND THE CARRIAGE, CATTLE, OR OTHER ANIMALS UNDER HIS CARE, HAVE PASSED THROUGH THE SAME, HE SHALL FORFEIT FOR EVERY SUCH OFFENCE ANY SUM NOT EXCEEDING **FORTY SHILLINGS.**"

EUSTON STATION,
1ST NOVEMBER, 1883.

BY ORDER.

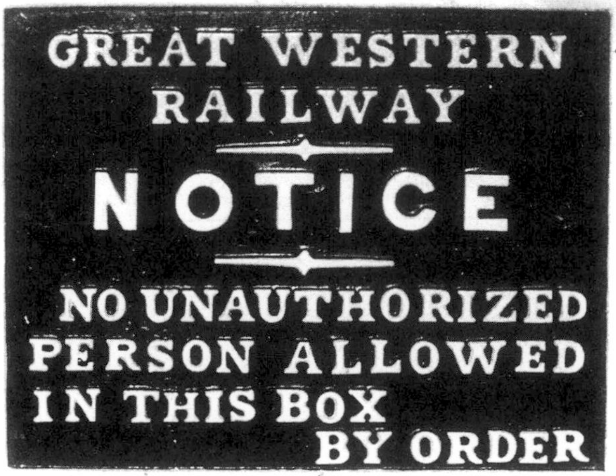

GREAT WESTERN RAILWAY

NOTICE

NO UNAUTHORIZED PERSON ALLOWED IN THIS BOX

BY ORDER

This page:
London & North Western Railway 'gate' notice. It is untypical, for such signs are usually much simpler. Winchcombe Railway Museum.
Very popular among collectors is the GWR signal box notice. Variations are found on the GW & LNW Joint, Severn & Wye Joint and West London Extension Railways. Graham Thomas Collection.
Opposite page:
A bridge notice from the Cambrian Railways, providing some very precise if perplexing information as to the limits of the bridge. Winchcombe Railway Museum.

notice was provided by the GWR, warning of the 'dangerous practice of propping up the doors of merchandise trucks for the support of coal weighing machines'. The reason for the presence of this sign in the yard is worth explaining. Many accidents had been caused by the failure of poles that were often used to prop up wagon doors in the horizontal position whilst the contents, such as coal, were unloaded and weighed into bags. The GWR presumably wished to absolve themselves from any liability that might result from an accident caused by this practice–hence the notice was displayed in a prominent place in the goods yard.

Most of the big railway companies produced enamel versions of their familiar cast iron signs, though these are usually less well preserved. The enamel notices usually follow the general layout of their cast iron counterparts. However, as was mentioned earlier, some Scottish lines produced enamel signs only, whilst a few of the smaller English companies, such as Wirral Railway did likewise.

Most railway companies producing public notices also provided bridge number plates and boundary posts. Bridges were numbered for easy identification by company servants. Usually they bear the initials of the owning railway rather than its full title. Most are oval, though rectangular ones also occur. Some companies produced only bridge plates and no other notices at all. Such were the Cockermouth, Keswick and Penrith and the Cleater & Workington Junction railways, and their bridge plates are consequently highly sought after.

Boundary posts are used to identify a railway company's boundary when the extremities of it are not immediately obvious. They can usually be found on land bordering stations. Sometimes they can be quite a distance from the railway itself which indicates that the company owns extensive property. Often boundary posts would be placed between railway land and that of a factory with private sidings in which case they would be located between the adjacent tracks. The variety of design in boundary posts makes them interesting relics to collect. Some are several feet in length with a considerable proportion buried in the ground, like the LSWR examples. Some, like those made for Cambrian Railways are only a few

MOTOR CAR ACTS 1896 AND 1903.

NOTICE.

THIS BRIDGE IS INSUFFICIENT TO CARRY A HEAVY MOTOR CAR, THE REGISTERED AXLE WEIGHT OF ANY AXLE OF WHICH EXCEEDS THREE TONS, OR THE REGISTERED AXLE WEIGHTS OF THE SEVERAL AXLES OF WHICH EXCEED IN THE AGGREGATE FIVE TONS. OR A HEAVY MOTOR CAR DRAWING A TRAILER, IF THE REGISTERED AXLE WEIGHTS OF THE SEVERAL AXLES OF THE HEAVY MOTOR CAR AND THE AXLE WEIGHTS OF THE SEVERAL AXLES OF THE TRAILER EXCEED IN THE AGGREGATE FIVE TONS.
CAMBRIAN RAILWAYS COMPANY.
S. WILLIAMSON,
SECRETARY. OSWESTRY. SALOP.

SHROPSHIRE UNION RAILWAYS
& CANAL COMPANY
NOTICE
THIS PATH ON SUFFERANCE ONLY

CYCLING ON THE COMPANYS TOWING
PATH IS STRICTLY PROHIBITED
3.1901   BY ORDER

LANCASHIRE & YORKSHIRE RAILWAY Co.

NOTICE.

MECHANICALLY DRIVEN JIGGERS

AND FRICTION CRANES.

IN WORKING MECHANICALLY DRIVEN JIGGERS AND
FRICTION CRANES, GREAT CARE MUST BE USED IN
PUTTING THEM IN MOTION, SO AS TO PREVENT
JERKING THE CHAINS OR ROPES AGAINST THE
PILLARS OR JIBS.

An interesting double notice from the Shropshire Union Railways & Canal Company. Trespass and bridge notices from this company have rounded corners with the beading set in from the edge. Winchcombe Railway Museum.

The Lancashire & Yorkshire Railway are known for their wide variety of notices, this example being for the attention of company servants. It is to be found fastened to goods shed walls. Graham Thomas Collection.

inches long. As in the case of bridge plates there were some companies which only produced boundary posts. They were usually small lines, such as the Alexandra Newport & South Wales Docks & Railway Company.

An important question facing collectors of public notices is in what colours to paint them when they are restored. The external appearance of the sign when it is obtained often gives no clue. If the layers of paint are carefully scraped off, the original coat can sometimes be seen. Most companies used either a white background for their cast iron notices with black letters and beading (CLC), or a black background with white letters and beading (GWR). There was, unfortunately, little variation between these two styles. Evidence suggests that the GC&Mid.Joint used a blue background with white letters for their notices and the Great Eastern may have done so as well. M&GN fire bucket notices are often found with red backgrounds and black letters which seems to be original and also quite logical. The LSWR is considered to have given its notices a red background and white letters. However, apart from these and a few other odd cases, most cast iron signs were basically black and white.

Enamel notices tended to be a little more colourful; many companies favoured a blue background with white letters, the Furness Railway being one such line. The GNSR enamel notices have an off-white background with brown letters and are rather attractive when in good condition.

The actual collection of these notices is usually done on site. British Rail frequently sell notices and allow them to be removed by the purchaser. Collectors' Corner, run by BR, and shops specialising in relics, often have some for sale at a few pounds each. This, for many collectors, is their great attraction for quite large displays can be built up comparatively cheaply. However, as in most cases of supply and demand, rare notices exchange hands for considerable sums of money.

A boundary post from the Midland Railway made from a piece of rail with an oval plate welded on to it. The cast, hollow-backed letters are attached by brass rivets. Winchcombe Railway Museum.

A bridge plate from the Cockermouth, Keswick & Penrith Railway. Although a typical oval plate, it is a rare example from this line. Despite the high number made, few survive because the LMS and later BR replaced most of them. Graham Thomas Collection.

Maps

David Garnett

In the two decades following the opening of the Liverpool and Manchester Railway in 1830, there was an unprecedented rise in the demand for maps. At the same time, the planners of railways whittled away the resources of map makers for making up-to-date maps. Journeys that had so recently involved much preparation and no little heart-searching and had often taken several days, with nights in strange beds, could now be undertaken, with nonchalence, almost without preparation and in time measured in hours, not days. An appetite for travel was awakened. People realised they could now quite easily travel for business or pleasure and remote sounding places seemed less remote. A map was needed to see just where those places were and how best to get there and the map makers throve.

There was, however, a snag. Competent map draughtsmen and surveyors were rare and accurate surveying instruments even rarer. By 1830, the published one-inch Ordnance Survey maps had barely covered that part of England south and east of a line from Bristol to Hull. The first sheet had been published on January 1st, 1801, but thereafter niggardly finance, shortage of competent surveyors and equipment, and a rather pressing need to produce accurate maps of Ireland had delayed progress. Not for nearly another forty years was all England and Wales to be covered by one-inch maps. Six-inch maps of Lancashire and Yorkshire began to appear in the 1840s but the 25-inch series, so desirable for railway planners, first appeared in the 1850s and took some thirty years to cover England and Wales.

Meanwhile the railway planners had to make their own plans. Surveyors were at a premium and anyone who had ever held a chain aspired to the title 'surveyor'. The commercial map sellers had to make do with what they had until the Ordnance Survey sheets became available. Apart from railways and canals, the topographical features of the land changed but slowly, so maps based on surveys of the past could be sold with minimal or no corrections, provided the railways could be shown.

It is worth digressing for a moment to consider the position before the advent of the Ordnance Survey. Early 'picture' maps have no place here but it is not without interest to note that John Ogilby (1600–1676) published in 1675 an atlas of the most beautiful strip road maps covering all roads of importance in England and Wales. These were the equivalent of present date route maps as issued by the Automobile Association but beautifully hand coloured. Until that time, map makers had not bothered much about roads. Thereafter they became an important feature. Ogilby's route maps were adapted for railway travellers in some of the guides of the late 1830s and, in 1846, the *Railway Chronicle* produced a whole series of folding charts showing features of interest on either side of the line. More recently the Great Northern Railway and its successor produced similar charts of the East Coast Route under the title *On Either Side*. Both the Great Western and the London, Midland and Scottish Railways produced similar route books whilst S. N. Pike produced one for the Southern Railway, as well as for

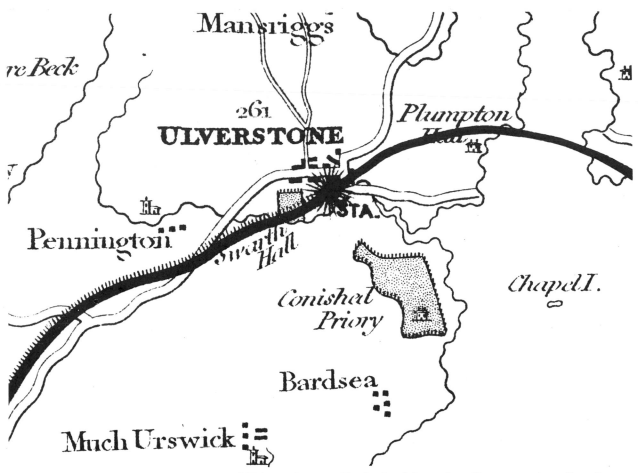

Detail from G. F. Cruchley's 'Railway and Telegraphic Map of Westmoreland' showing how the telegraph route was indicated, following the railway line. David Garnett Collection.

the London and North Eastern and LMS Railways.

But to return to general maps; triangulation had been in use by map makers for nearly three centuries. This was the process whereby the position of a landmark, visible from two positions a known distance apart, could be plotted with accuracy, even without going there. 'Accuracy' was relevant to the times and tended to diminish as the area involved increased. Jesse Ramsden, 1735–1800, a Yorkshireman then considered to be the most skilful instrument maker in the world, produced, in 1787, a theodolite with a horizontal scale three feet in diameter and capable of measuring angles to tenths of a second. This was in regular use by the Ordnance Survey for over sixty years. He also made superior chains and even long glass tubes as measures of length. Aaron Arrowsmith, 1750–1823, using the best methods and instruments available, surveyed Scotland for a map produced in the early thirties. The known inaccuracies of this were being used to press for completion of an Ordnance Survey of Scotland only twenty years later.

The basis of the early railway maps was, therefore, a topographical map of uncertain age and accuracy, though these were increasingly advertised as 'Corrected from the Ordnance Survey' as this became available. Some were beautifully engraved on copper. George Bradshaw, 1801–1853, of timetable fame, was an apprentice engraver who took to maps as the best media for his skill and artistic temperament. It is thought that he added letterpress printing to his business with a view to creating an outlet for his maps by publishing railway timetables. His maps were always creditable. On March 23rd, 1840, George Frederick Cruchley published a gigantic *Map of the Railways, showing the various stations with the hills, rivers, canals and principal roads, of England and Wales, also exhibiting most of the places whose situation has been ascertained by the Stations and Intersections of the Trigonometrical Survey, compiled by A. Arrowsmith, Hydrographer to His Majesty.* The map was to a scale of 6 miles to an inch and was on four large sheets folding into a case. It had much topographical detail and railways were shown by a curious symbol like a ladder with one side removed! County boundaries were colour washed with different colours for each side. Railways were also coloured with a thin line of colour applied by hand. Solid red showed railways completed, dotted red

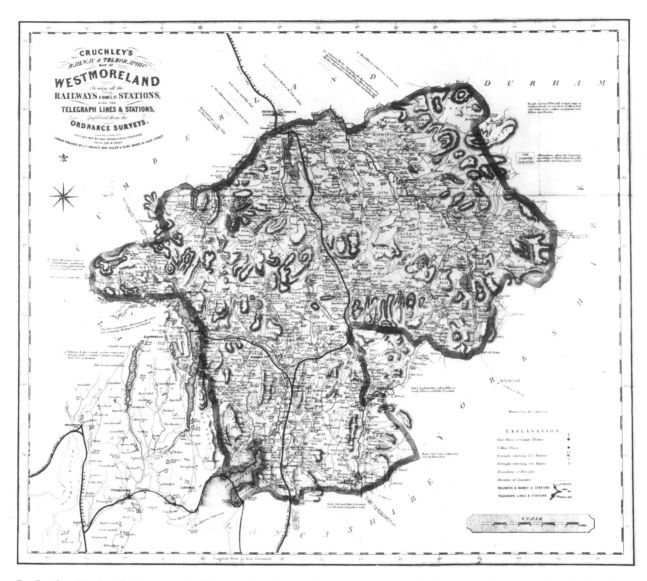

G. F. Cruchley's 'Railway and Telegraphic Map of Westmoreland' dated (bottom left) January 1st, 1856. David Garnett Collection.

railways in progress and solid blue railways projected. Periodic reprints were made, eg one with 'Additions to 1845'. These appear to be the same base map with just the hand colouring to show additional railways completed or started or projected. Mr Cruchley, like many after him, was quite content to show lines meeting at right angles when he did not know which way the junction faced!

From about 1855 onward, Cruchley produced a most interesting series of county maps, the scale of which varied from about 2½ to 6½ miles to the inch, apparently in an effort to standardise the sheet size. The earlier maps of this series were called *Cruchley's Railway and Telegraphic Map of . . .*, and a few were dated. Later the title became *Cruchley's Railway and Station Map of . . .*, and ultimately *Cruchley's County Map of. . . .* An inter-

esting feature of these maps is the emphasis placed on showing telegraph routes. The telegraph was, of course, developed by the railway companies for their own use but it also became a useful source of income. Until teleprinters and underground cables took over, trunk telegraph lines continued to be provided by main line railway companies.

Another important series of maps was provided by Charles Frederick Cheffins. Cheffins described himself as a lithographer but seems to have been fascinated by railways, of which he produced a considerable number of maps between about 1835 and 1848. Some of his maps were dated but, like so many others, he found it best not to put a date on maps whilst developments were taking place so fast. His later maps of England and Wales, which ran to several editions, had hand coloured additions as lines were opened. One of his earliest maps was *London and Birmingham Railway. Plan of the Line and Adjacent Country. 1835.* A little gem is his *Map of the Railway from London to Boxmoor and the Adjacent Country* published in August, 1837. *Cheffin's Official Map of the London & Birmingham Railway and the Adjacent Country. 1837* shows the railway route between London and Birmingham but also shows the road from Denbigh Hall to Rugby, coloured blue. It includes tables of fares and the distances of various places from the nearest station.

A series of maps which painfully high-light the dangers besetting anyone buying a map by post is J. & C. Walker's *County Maps.* These range between about 1835 and 1870 and are handsome little maps, usually cloth mounted and folded in hard covers of pocket size. The snag is that many of them have a table of towns showing their population in 1841. This is sometimes quoted by booksellers as the date of the map. Many such show the railways as they were up to thirty years later! This series is also of interest for the variety of symbols used on the lithograph to indicate railways, presumably open, under construction or authorised, but seldom with any explanation. These were over-coloured by hand to show routes at the time of issue and many such are merely lines of colour with nothing

on the lithograph.

In the last two decades of the 19th century, W. H. Smith & Son, of bookstall fame, produced a series of pocket maps covering much of England and Wales. They were fully coloured, cloth mounted and cloth cased and sold for 1/– each. The *Liverpool Albion* became quite lyrical about them. 'These splendid Maps, unquestionably the most perfect ever published, have been compiled from the Ordnance and Admiralty Surveys, with Railways up to the latest date. Their particulars are most minute and accurate; and every possible information that a map can give is afforded'. After that no one will be surprised to learn that the maps were prepared by John Bartholomew. The scale was usually four miles to the inch and the title, in most cases, incorporated the words 'and Environs', eg *Leeds and Environs* or *Gloucester, Cheltenham and Environs.* The maps are undated. A casual look at one of these

---

Detail from C. F. Cheffins's 'Map of the Railway from London to Box Moor and the Adjacent Country'. Dated August 1st, 1837. David Garnett Collection.

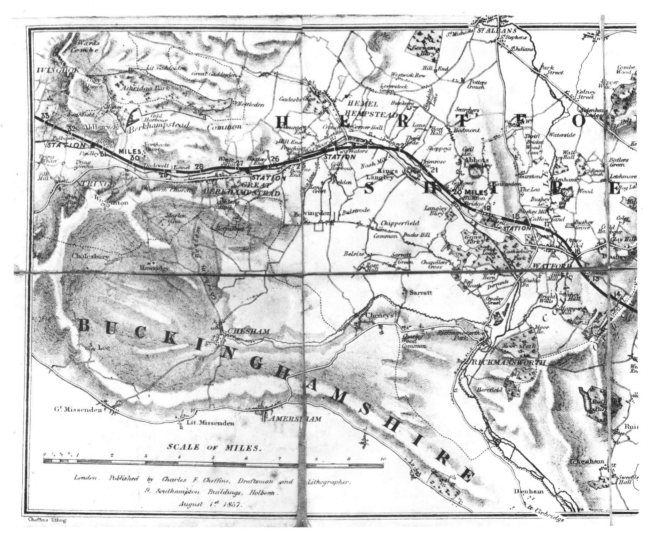

maps leaves one in full agreement with the *Liverpool Albion* reviewer. A closer look reveals much of interest to the ferro-equestrian cartophile in the way of proposed railways, which are shown in very fine triple parallel lines in sweeping curves which the eye does not immediately pick out against the background of roads.

The writer's copy of *Gloucester, Cheltenham and Environs* shows a projected end-on connection between the Malmesbury and Nailsworth branches and one with right-angled junctions between the Midland line just south of Standish and the South Wales line after crossing the Severn near Arlingham. It also shows a projected line between Caerleon and Usk. The engraver had a better eye for curves than for civil engineering plausibility though his 'as built' lines, shown by a thick line with a thin one on each side, are reasonably accurate for the scale of map. An even closer study of this map, as of some others in the series, shows projected routes which have been abandoned but imperfectly deleted from the engraving. The route is deleted completely from open spaces but not at all where deletion would damage other words or features of the map and the whole route can be traced from these remains. An early form of the South Wales Direct line is shown thus: it leaves the Great Western main line in the 'as built' position just west of Wootton Bassett but then runs increasingly to the north of the 'as built' route, being to the north of Brinkworth and Little Somerford, crossing the Malmesbury Branch at Cowbridge, close to Malmesbury, running to the north of Sherston and just to the south of Didmarton, skirting Badminton Park on its north side, thence north of Thornbury, crossing the Severn as though it was dry land and finally making a right-angled junction with the South Wales line just north of Sedbury. The Thornbury branch is shown extended to make a right-angled junction and there is a line, still fully shown, from Pilning to another right-angled junction on the east bank of the river. Truly a fascinating series of maps, now rather rare.

The promoters of a new railway, seeking Parliamentary powers to acquire land and build their railway, had to comply with extensive Standing Orders. Among other requirements were maps to a scale of one inch to a mile showing the approximate route and plans to a scale of not less than four inches to a mile. These maps and plans had to be supplied, gratis, to all the public bodies concerned as well as to all and sundry directly concerned with the Parliamentary Bill. Copies of plans deposited with the local Clerk of the Peace were sealed and many such are in County Archive Offices, still sealed, though seals have been broken increasingly as time passes and these old plans are of great interest. They are not common in private collections and are bulky things to store. The maps were usually over-

printed or hand drawn on the current Ordnance Survey one-inch sheets. They were often mounted on cloth and sometimes bound in hard cases of leather or cloth board and are occasionally to be found with a title gold-blocked on the front. Where the proposed new railway covered a long distance it became necessary to mount several sheets together, especially in the case of the quarter sheets of the Second Edition and Small Sheets of the Third Edition. This work was often undertaken by James Wyld or his successor, Edward Stanford, and bear their labels.

The statutory requirements for the Parliamentary Plans were laid down very fully. Apart from the minimum scale mentioned above, enlargements at not less than one inch to 400 feet had to be made of any building, yard or garden within the limits of deviation permitted from the proposed centre line of the railway. These limits were specified as ten yards in built-up areas or not more than 100 yards elsewhere. A longitudinal section at a scale of not less than one inch to 100 feet was also required and this had to show every cutting or embankment more than five feet high as well as every crossing of a public highway, navigable river, canal or other railway. Moreover, if the level of any such existing right of way was proposed to be altered an enlargement was required at a scale of not less than one inch to 330 feet horizontally and one inch to 40 feet vertically. The plans had to show every parcel of land within the limits of deviation. Every such parcel was numbered and a book of reference had to be prepared to show the owner and occupier thereof. The plans were usually engraved and then printed by lithography and the Books of Reference were also printed. It is hardly surprising that the Parliamentary cost of obtaining an Act for building a railway were so astronomical. Promoters of railways often produced sketch maps of the proposed route and these were usually incorporated in prospectuses sent to potential supporters. Like much promotion material these prospectuses are now very rare but can be of immense interest, not least if the scheme was abandoned.

Among the most interesting of maps to the railway enthusiast are those prepared by railwaymen for railwaymen. Once a railway was built, most of the topographical features of commercially produced maps were of no interest to railwaymen. They wanted to know the relative positions of stations, the location of junctions, the ownership of lines and the mileages from point to point. One of the first attempts to meet these requirements was made by Zachary Macaulay, a clerk in the employ of the Railway Clearing House. He compiled a map of the railways of Great Britain in 1849 which he hoped to get officially published. However the prospects did not appeal to his employers but later, whilst still employed by the Railway Clearing House,

Midland Railway poster map, c. 1911. National Railway Museum.

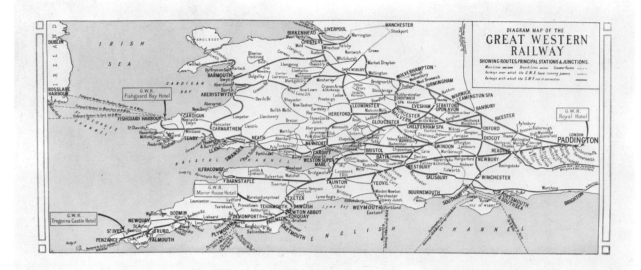

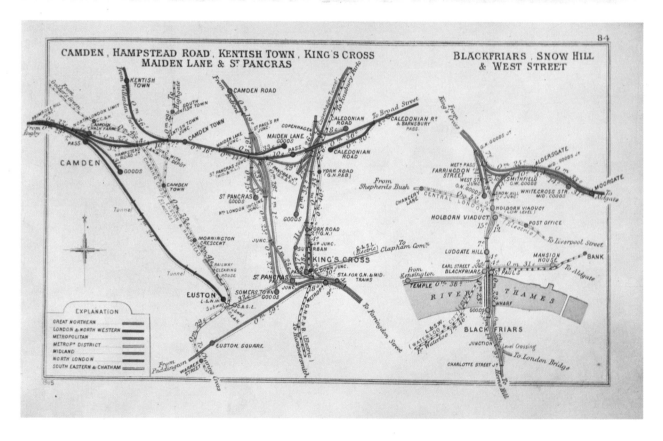

GWR carriage panel map. These were exhibited in the centre panel above the seats, flanked by photographs. This is a later version of the Emery Walker map.

Railway Clearing House Junction Diagram Map clearly showing the junctions of the pre-grouping railways in the area concerned. 1915. P. B. Whitehouse Collection.

he had his map printed by Smith and Ebbs and published it himself on 28 January 1851. In a catalogue for 1893, Mr Edward Baker, the once famous Birmingham bookseller, described this map as follows: 'This is far the most attractive map of the date not only showing the Stations but marking all the different lines in different colours'. He offered a copy for 21 shillings. The title of Macaulay's map was *Macaulay's Station Map of the Railways of Great Britain*. It was a large map, to a scale of ten miles to an inch. It was sold mounted on rollers but is usually found dissected, mounted on cloth and bound bookform into covers measuring about 9in by 5¾in. Most are covered with a purplish cloth which has become very fragile with age so that many copies exist without the front cover. Macaulay took pride in making it clear that his map was 'Corrected by the Companies', but neither he nor they were averse to showing right-angled junctions. The railway routes are hand coloured and there is a pleasing coastal wash of blue. Copies mounted and bound by commercial map-sellers are known, eg Stanford and Letts. A copy with the counties coloured has been seen.

The first four editions were boldly dated under the title: 1851, 1852, 1854 and 1856. 1852 has 'Second Edition' under the date. 1854 and 1856 both have 'Third Edition' under the date, but the latter has been extensively updated. There were nineteen further editions up to and including 1893, after which the map ceased publication. The fifth edition has no date or edition number but the sixth, published in 1860, has a small edition number just inside the margin lines in the top left-hand corner. This edition number, with two eccentricities, survived up to the last edition, number 22. For the fifteenth edition, in 1877, Macaulay must have rethought his belief that dating a map was disadvantageous to sales. Perhaps he realised that buyers wanted to be sure they were buying an up-to-date map and were not prepared to be fobbed off with an 'attractive' map of uncertain vintage. Anyway he reverted to dating his maps in 1877 but put the date rather unobtrusively in a position corresponding to the edition number but in the top right-hand corner or, in one or two cases, about four inches further down. Two eccentricities in edition numbers are mentioned above. One is that the 19th edition, of 1884, is numbered '18a'. A '19' edition, of 1886, is actually entered on the Stationers' Hall Register but no copy is known to the writer. Edition number 20, of 1888, and number 22, of 1893, are both 'above board', but the intermediate edition of 1891 is actually numbered '15'. The serious student of these and other maps may well be confounded one day by finding two apparently identical editions with differences—not just differences in the hand colouring, which are common, but differences on the lithograph. The writer, who has made no intensive

study of Macaulay's Great Britain as yet, knows of two variations of the fifth, and two of the seventh, editions.

Macaulay must have been pleased with the reception of his map because he published on 20 October, 1859, *Macaulay's Metropolitan Railway Map*. This was a nice little map, measuring about 21in by 16½in and usually dissected, mounted and folded, like its larger companion, into hard covers about 6¼in by 4½in. The scale was two miles to an inch and the direction in which junctions faced was usually correctly shown. The title is deceptive. This is a map of the railways of the Metropolis, not just of The Metropolitan Railway. There were eleven editions up to and including 1875, by which time the map was probably eclipsed by that of John Airey mentioned below. No edition was dated, but all except the first had the edition number in the top left-hand corner. No copy of the 9th edition is known to the writer but he has found three variants of the first edition and four of the second. Macaulay died in 1860 and the copyright of his two maps passed to his widow. However, in 1863, Smith and Ebbs produced *Station Map of the Railways of Ireland* (A companion to the Station Map of Great Britain designed by Z. Macaulay). This ran to sixteen editions by 1907 but there was a 4a edition in 1875. From the sixth edition, of 1879, onwards, the maps were dated like the later ones of Great Britain. None of these maps showed point-to-point mileages.

In 1852 a young man by the name of John Airey joined the staff of the Railway Clearing House and was allocated to the Distances Department. Here he helped with the gigantic task of reckoning the exact mileage between every station and siding in the country, to enable through rates and fares to be calculated, and allocated between the Companies if more than one was involved. As the railway system grew, the task must have become colossal and it was essential to know the precise point where one company's metals gave way to another. There was, in the office, a set of hand drawn and coloured diagrams to show the more important junctions and these were re-drawn, or added to, as necessary, when new lines were opened. It must have occurred to John Airey, or perhaps to his Departmental Chief, Henry Oliver, that such diagrams would be useful to railwaymen in general, not least as showing if through running without reversal at junctions was possible. Accordingly, in January 1867, John Airey published *Railway Junction Diagrams. Complete Work. Prepared from Official Drawings by John Airey and Corrected by the Companies. Price 10s. 6d.* It has never been explained how Airey ran a flourishing private enterprise, using official information, from his employers' address and in their time! The first Junction Diagram book had 84 diagram sheets measuring 10in by 8¼in bound, oblong, with an index. Each year, in Janu-

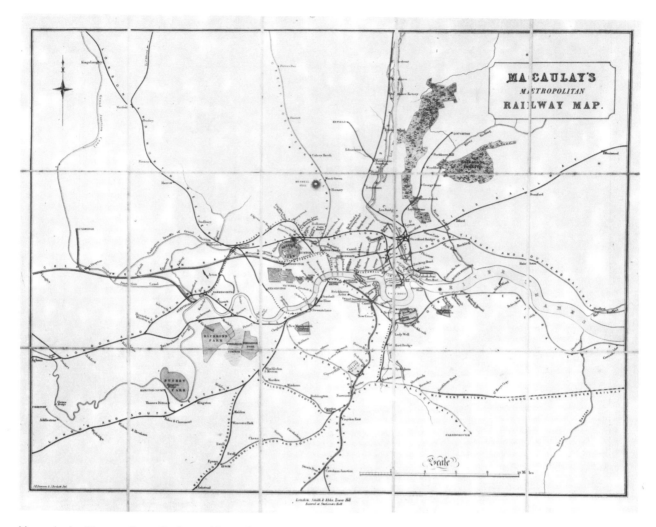

Macaulay's Metropolitan Railway Map of 1859. First version. David Garnett Collection.

ary, Airey published a Supplement for one shilling which contained new diagrams and replacements for those which had been altered. Early diagrams were hand coloured but for the Sixth Edition, of 1888, colour lithography was used throughout.

In the months following publication of the first Junction Diagram book, Airey must have realised the shortcomings of having Altrincham on one sheet, Manchester proper on another and Stalybridge on another, so early in 1869 he produced *Diagram of Manchester and District* to a scale of one inch to one mile and on a sheet measuring 22½in by 15¼in. He must have also realised that this would be saleable on its own so he went through copyright procedure for this sheet as he had for the full set in 1867. It was actually entered at Stationers' Hall on 28 April 1869 and was stated to have been published by John Airey on 15 April 1869. This enlarged diagram was the first of a long series of maps with which, by the time of his retirement, Airey had covered the whole of Great Britain except for Central and North Wales.

On 4 November 1869 Airey published *Railway Diagram of London and its Suburbs* and on 5 October 1870, *Railway Diagram of South Wales*. On 20 November 1871, *Railway Map of the Yorkshire District* followed, and the title 'Map' was adopted in place of 'Diagram' and the earlier ones were altered as they were revised.

None of Airey's maps was dated until January 1876 and, in addition to the three mentioned above, each with several revisions, undated copies of his maps of Lancashire, Staffordshire and Scotland are known. All others are dated, with the month and year for the early part of 1876 but with the year only thereafter. Airey successively produced maps covering the following areas: Durham & Northumberland, Derbyshire & Nottinghamshire, Cumberland & Westmorland, South of England, West of England, East of England, Gloucestershire & Oxfordshire. Except for the last mentioned, several, or numerous, editions of different dates exist. Fifteen years ago the writer compiled a list of all known editions of Airey's maps for the Journal of the Railway and Canal Historical Society. There were 119. Now 158 are known, including variants of the same edition, but there are still some gaps which are too big to be credible. Some maps were revised every year whilst railways in their area were proliferating, eg London from 1875 to 1884 inclusive, but there are gaps as long on others though 'unknown' ones are reported from time to time. It is unfortunate that there is no official record of all editions and as it is known that only 100 copies of some editions were printed, the chance of at least one surviving where it can become known is not very great. Airey did not deposit copies with Copyright Offices after the first edition.

One of Airey's maps is really outside the series mentioned above. This is his *Railway Map of England and Wales*. This was actually published on 14 November 1876 but was dated 'January, 1877'. The scale was 1:712,800 or about 11¼ miles to an inch and it was the only one of Airey's maps which did not show point-to-point mileages. The map was published by McCorquodale & Co, who were joint owners of the copyright and probably commissioned it to compete with Macaulay's map, published by Smith & Ebbs, who were McCorquodale's chief competitor in printing for the railways. This map was no credit at all either to Airey or to McCorquodale. It was lithographed in black only, the different Railway Companies being differentiated by chains of dots, dashes, circles, crosses and so forth. The effect was not pleasing and the map was dropped next year for a hand coloured one similar to Airey's other maps, prepared and lithographed by J. Emslie & Sons. However, in 1881, the map was redesigned and lithographed in colour. It was now a great credit to all concerned and, with periodic revisions, continued in print to 1926.

Airey sold his business and stock to the Railway Clearing House in 1895, except for the England and Wales map which they acquired in October 1901, after a disastrous attempt to produce their own by reduction from a larger one they had commissioned meanwhile. The Railway Clearing House set about removing Airey's name from his plates and substituting a title incorporating the words *Official Railway Map of. . . .* Some of the maps published in 1896, 1897 and 1898 have old titles, some have transition titles in which 'by John Airey' remains, and some have new 'Official' titles with no mention of Airey.

The Railway Clearing House immediately commissioned a new map of Scotland at a scale of 7½ miles to an inch and a new one of England and Wales to the same scale. The former was less than half the scale of Airey's map and point-to-point mileages were left out. This latter was to a larger scale than Airey's and considerably bulkier. Both are superb examples of cartographic art. They were engraved by J. P. Emslie, son of the James Emslie who had engraved and lithographed all Airey's maps, but they were now lithographed in

colour by McCorquodale. A similar map of Ireland, to the same scale, followed in 1897 and a new map of *Edinburgh & Glasgow District* at a scale of two miles to an inch appeared next year. Thereafter the maps were gradually redrawn in the new style. The last appeared in 1914. Finally, *Glasgow, Coatbridge & Paisley* appeared in 1932, superseding *Edinburgh & Glasgow*. but J. P. Emslie had passed on and the style is quite different and the draughtsman remains anonymous. 182 editions of the twenty-one Railway Clearing House maps are known up to nationalisation and only one ('Scotland 1960') has appeared since.

Many of the Railway Companies had their own 'System Maps' designed to show their area of influence with important features therein. Most of them showed collieries and works with private sidings but point-to-point mileages were not usual. Some gave the 'home' line in colour with 'foreign' lines in black or sometimes in other colours with running powers indicated thereon. Quite a number of them are beautiful examples of utilitarian cartography and they were often mounted and folded into pleasing covers, sometimes with the name of the official to whom it was issued gold-blocked thereon. Some of these maps incorporated gradient diagrams though the larger companies usually produced these quite separately. Not all these maps were pleasing to behold and maps reproduced by a dyeline process, mounted and bound, are to be found occasionally.

The line of demarcation between maps intended primarily for internal use and those produced for free distribution to valued customers or for sale to the public, is rather thin. The North Eastern Railway produced a very large 'Products Map' in 1910, which may well have been designed as a poster but was also mounted and folded into hard covers. By a system of coloured squares and other symbols and lists, both natural and manufactured or imported product sources were represented over their whole sphere of influence. The Lancashire and Yorkshire Railway produced a number of maps and plans of docks and large cities which were folded into limp cloth covers of foolscap size. The Great Central Railway produced a spectacular 'bird's eye view' of the new Immingham docks, together with rail access plans. These are typical of many advertising maps.

The poster type of map has already been mentioned and there were a great many of these, issued by various companies, for exhibition on hoardings at stations and elsewhere. Some were straightforward system maps but others were embellished with idealistic views of watering places, places of scenic beauty or historical interest and sites suitable for Works. Being cumbersome and on cheap paper, few have survived unless also supplied mounted and folded.

The railway companies provided maps in their time-tables but these seldom competed with the simple beauty of Bradshaw's maps. Usually they were diagrammatic maps with a heavy emphasis on any advantage the company claimed for its routes over those of rivals. Prior to the Grouping of railways, such maps also appeared framed in railway compartments. During the first decade of this century, the Great Western Railway spent a vast sum of money on shortening its routes to Birmingham, South Wales and Devon by building more direct lines linking places otherwise reached only by more roundabout routes. Prior to this, 'wags' had interpreted GWR as 'Great Way Round'! So, on completion of the cut-offs, the company commissioned Emery Walker to design a map to defeat this image. His map showed the GWR in sweeping curves of such large radius as to approach straight lines. The effect was intensified by shortening the North to South scale relative to the East to West scale. These maps were really rather beautiful even if obviously exaggerated, and the idea spread to other companies who tended to stylise their maps thus.

A very important series of poster maps was that produced by the Metropolitan District Railway Company. These showed the 'District Railway' superimposed on a street plan and someone must have realised very quickly that such a map, if folded into covers, would find a ready sale. There was a whole series of these maps which sold for sixpence or a shilling if mounted on cloth before folding. With minor variations of title, they were available from 1873 to 1907. A new edition was produced whenever there was an extension to the District Railway but the street plan was often well out of date in detail and several variants of what purports to be same edition are known.

The Underground group of companies produced a beautiful little diagrammatic map of their lines in colour on cloth backed card, measuring about 6in by 4¼in when open and 2in by 4¼in when folded for the pocket. They also produced larger versions for issue to hotels, either as a semi-stiff folder or framed for hanging. The current London Transport pocket route diagrams are highly creditable for their simplification of a complicated system and have considerable utilitarian beauty.

Commercial cartographers have not neglected railways and have now lived down the poor image related earlier. Prior to the Nationalisation of Railways, the Ordnance Survey produced a splendid version of their two-sheet ten-miles-to-the-inch map overprinted with the railways. Then there was *Bartholomew's Railway Map of the British Isles* on a scale of 19 miles to the inch. This ran to several editions following Grouping. Stanford produced a number of railway maps including one measuring 11ft 10½in by 9ft 8in! Most of the commercial cartographers tackled this market at some time or another and produced maps of individuality for an area or for Great Britain as a whole. Indeed much of the interest to be had from railway maps lies in the great variety. Variety of purpose for which the map was prepared and variety in the way this purpose was fulfilled. Obsolete maps have always tended to be useless and to be thrown out or used as playthings or have been defaced by crude additions of lines since built. Inevitably they are acquiring a rarity value. Not all maps were deposited in Copyright Offices so the real enthusiast might consider making his gems available to fellow enthusiasts by leaving them to some reputable Museum, Library or Archive office in his Will.

In conclusion, one or two of the writer's little gems may be mentioned. *Philips' Cyclists Map of the Country of Wiltshire*, one of a large series of undated maps produced about the turn of the century, shows, as a fait accompli, 'Even Swindon Sta.'. This was shown on the Midland and South Western Junction Railway, about half way between the points where it crossed the Great Western main line and the Cheltenham line. An old local resident remembers walking across the fields with his father, a local Councillor, to look at the proposed site. The station was never built. The area called Even (ie level) Swindon is to the west of the Cheyney Manor estate. Another interesting map, probably rather rare, is made up from the original Ordnance Survey ten-miles-to-the-inch map, South Sheet, which was prepared as an index to the original one-inch maps. Someone must have bought a number and had them dissected and mounted into cloth boards measuring 8⅛in by 5in and gold embossed *Western Railways 1846*. On the map face, lines 'For which Acts are obtained' are shown in solid colour for the Great Western, South Western and Taw Vale lines, whilst in dotted colour are shown 'Lines of 1846: Projected by Great Western (blue); Bristol and Exeter (green) and South Western (red)'. There is no indication as to by whom or for whom the map was prepared but an interesting feature is the method of adding the colour. It would appear that the route to be coloured was first marked on the map surface by two small sharp wheels which have incised twin lines about 1mm apart. The space between the lines has been filled very thickly with colour, either solid lines or dotted, and the effect is rather like of the machines which paint yellow or white lines on roadways! The colour stands proud and there is an extra blob at the beginning or end sometimes. The writer has not seen this process elsewhere.

Contemplation of an old map is fascinating and restful, even if it begets an urge to get up and go and see for oneself. A new acquisition is always thrilling, sometimes disappointing and often a source of friction with the Bank Manager!

Bartholomew's Railway Map of the British Isles, dated 1927. There were earlier editions of this post-grouping map. LMS lines are shown in red, LNER in green, GWR in mauve and SR in brown. David Garnett Collection.

Signals and Signalling Equipment

F. B. Gell

Signalling has always had a fascination all its own. Probably many of the people who collect pieces of signal equipment today have been swayed by the magic of the block instruments' tinkling bells, or the thought of those shining levers controlling all movements on adjacent tracks. An excellent book on the subject is L. T. C. Rolt's *Red for Danger*, which records not only some of the appalling disasters in British railway history, but also traces the positive achievement of safety on the line from the days of the hand signalling 'policeman' to the automatic train control equipment of today. The last decade, with its fast Inter City electric trains, running at average speeds only dreamed of in the age of steam, has swept away some of the glamour of the old-fashioned signalling systems, but much of the equipment still lives on in its original form on our tourist railway and in the hands of private collectors.

The earliest form of control or signalling on the railway was the timetable. Trains were few in number, with low speeds and frequent stoppages. The timetable was arranged to keep the trains apart, ensure that they ran at fixed times, and allow staff along the line to prepare for their arrival. This soon became impracticable as the volume of traffic and the speed of the trains increased, and railway policemen were introduced at certain points where it could be necessary for trains to stop. These policemen in their top hats and swallowtail coats were stationed along the line to signal drivers to stop in unexpected circumstances. (Even today the signalman is nicknamed the 'bobby'.)

It soon became obvious that the most vigilant of policeman could not be in more than one place at a time, and so the first fixed signals were introduced. In the event these proved insufficient, and an additional signal was provided to give forewarning of a stop signal. These, known as auxiliary, or distant signals, were the forerunners of the distant signals of today. With the further increase in the number of trains and their differing speeds, the old timetable reckoning became often unreliable and dangerous. It was now necessary to prevent trains from overtaking each other, and so the 'Time Interval' system was initiated. The obvious limitations of this system soon became apparent and in about 1850 a 'Space Interval' system, worked by means of electrical apparatus was introduced. This was known as the 'Block System'.

One of the most appealing features of collecting signalling equipment is the wide variety of material available and, unlike some railwayana, it is both attractive and easy to display. The equipment can be divided into four main groups—signals, block instruments and signal box instruments, single line working, and printed matter relating to the subject.

Signals

One early form of signal was the disc and cross-bar, designed by Brunel and the first to give two positive directions. This signal was pivoted on the top of a post so that it could be turned through an angle of ninety degrees. To an oncoming train the cross-bar indicated stop and the disc all clear. So successful

LMS Preston No 1 signal box.

were they that they remained in operation on the GWR until the 1880s. More sophisticated signalling of the lower quadrant type was widely used in the 1850s and this was followed by upper quadrants, a type of semaphore signalling in which the arm was raised rather than lowered. These changes ensured that the signal 'failed safe'. The upper quadrant first appeared on the LMS during the 1930s.

Special signal boards used to control the entry to goods yards had a white ring at the end of the board, while a shunting signal had a capital letter S in a similar position. Other smaller types of shunting signals appeared either in the form of discs near ground level or miniature semaphore types. The ground disc signals were used to a great extent for shunting purposes at sidings and crossovers. Of particular interest to collectors are the signal post finials. Pre-grouping companies had their own designs and many now decorate the gardens of collectors.

Telegraph Instruments
The 'induced needle' basis of the single needle telegraph instrument was invented by C. E. Spagnoletti,

a railway superintendent with the Great Western in 1869. The needle was flicked from side to side by the operator's manipulation of the handle. The two white stops enabled the operator to read off the flicks left or right. Routine messages were condensed into code to save time. In the audible class is Bright's Bell instrument, invented by C. T. Bright (1832–88) with two differently-toned sounding plates struck by separate hammers. The Morse Code is used, but the signals are of equal duration, one tone representing a dot, the other a dash, the signals being read by listening to the difference of tone.

Block Signalling Instruments
The principle underlying this method of controlling the running of trains, is that no train is allowed to proceed from a station or other clearly defined point unless a certain definite length of clear track is known to exist ahead, limited by a signal of some sort. The complete equipment for one section consists at each end of a transmitting or 'pegger' instrument, a receiving or 'non pegger' instrument, and a block bell and key for transmitting and receiving of code signals.

There is only slight variation in the forms of instruments used for block signalling. They can be roughly

Left:
An old-fashioned disc signal in use on the Festiniog Railway in the 1960s, now in the Towyn Museum.
Below left:
Old signalling equipment put to good use today. Ex-GWR semaphore arms controlling the entrance to the Llanfair Caereinion station of the amateur-run Welshpool and Llanfair Light Railway.
Below:
A signal at Donegal town station from the County Donegal Railways Joint Committee. This signal is now on display at the Narrow Gauge Railway Museum at Towyn.

Block instruments in the No 1 Camden signal box, LMS Railway. Note that this is an electric box.

divided into two kinds, three wire block and one wire block (referring to the number of wires required to operate the instruments in one section), or two position and three position (referring to the number of indications shown).

They consist usually of some form of needle instrument, showing three indications: 'line clear' 'line blocked' and 'train on line'. An adaptation of this is Spagnoletti's disc block instrument, which was the standard block instrument used by the GWR. The indications are on small flags which show through an aperture in the case. Another variation is by a small semaphore giving only two indications 'line clear' and 'line blocked'.

The simplest form of three wire instrument was the one used on the Midland Railway, known as the 'Midland Pegger'. The handle is fixed in its position by a peg. Generally only the instrument at the leaving end of the section is fitted with a handle, as it is this signalman who controls the section, the instrument at the receiving end being fitted with a dial only. Preece's three wire instrument gives its indications

by means of a miniature semaphore, above this is a disc indicator showing the 'On' or 'Off' of the semaphore on the instrument at the other end of the section.

Of the one wire block instruments the principal types are the *Tyer, Walker, Harper Preece* and an improved *Sykes*. All are operated by momentary currents transmitted when bell signals are given, the indication being maintained until cancelled by another signal.

The *Walker* instrument was designed by C. V. Walker a telegraph engineer to the South Eastern Railway, and was first used on the opening of the Charing Cross Railway in 1864. It consists of a miniature signal post, with an arm for each direction, a bell mechanism, commutator, and a ringing plunger. Preece's instrument is similar to the three wire example, but without the safety feature. It is fitted with a lock which makes it necessary for both signalmen to co-operate in order to lower it to 'line clear'. With Tyer's (two position), one form is fitted with an additional disc indicator, another has no disc, but two plungers to control the indicators and a separate ringing plunger. Tyer's (three position) has three needle indications including 'line blocked'. The commutator handle can be fitted with a catch

Three examples of signal repeater. Left: LNWR with lamp in/out indicator; centre: LSWR type; right: a Tyer's repeater. F. B. Gell Collection.

lock to prevent the movements taking place in anything but the prescribed order. Sykes' three position has electrical principles derived from a one wire three position instrument designed by R. R. Harper in 1885. An added feature is an alarm which sounds at each end of the section should both signalmen ring at the same moment.

A bell or gong is provided in each box for giving the code signals necessary with block telegraph. They are operated either by a tapper key or a plunger, the tapper key often combined with the bell rung from the adjacent box. A number of block instruments include a bell and tapper key as in the LNWR standard instrument.

Permissive Block Working
Lines used exclusively for goods traffic and large stations where trains are connected together are often worked on the permissive block system. This allows trains to enter a section which is already occupied. Each train entering such a section is stopped and warned of the number of trains ahead of it. Special block instruments such as *Tyer's Patent Permissive Indicating Block Instrument* are fitted with an indicator registering the number of trains in the section.

Lock and Block
This system was introduced in an effort to overcome the element of human error. The signal for entering the section is interlocked with the block instrument so that the former cannot be lowered unless the latter shows 'line clear'. The main instruments are the *Sykes* and the *Rotary* or *Midland*. If a train has to be cancelled and the instrument reset, a key, as in the Sykes' Instrument, was provided which inserted in the instrument or contact box, released the instrument. With the *Midland* or *Rotary*, a button was provided at the bottom of the block behind glass.

Signal Repeaters
To ensure that the signalman knows a signal has responded to the movements of the lever, electrical signal repeaters are fitted into signal boxes. This instrument consists of an indicator with positions corresponding to the signal arm.

Lamp or Light Repeaters
For the same reasons that necessitate the signals being repeated in the signal box, the condition of the signal lamps must also be indicated. In some cases, as with the *Sykes' Arm and Lamp Repeater* the two are included in one instrument.

Occupation Keys
Made by Tyer's, this is a simple method of controlling

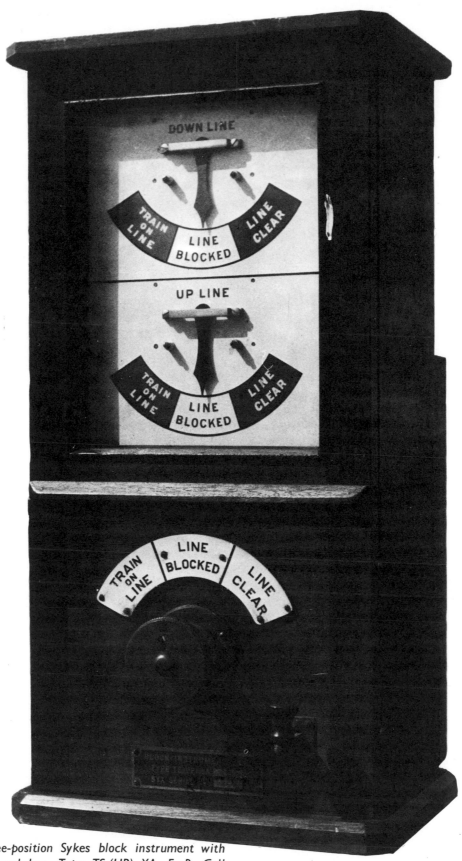

An early three-position Sykes block instrument with integral bell and key. Type TS.(UP) YA. F. B. Gell Collection.

A pair of Midland Railway instruments—the standard pegging type and a rotary block instrument made in 1910. F. B. Gell Collection.

branch lines and intermediate sidings, and also enables permanent way gangs to work on single lines without the protection of flagmen. The GWR had its own particular system known as the *Economic System of Maintenance*. This consisted of one instrument into which a key was locked at the signal box at each end of the section, and at as many places along the line as was necessary depending on the length of the section. The withdrawal of one key locked the other, and train token as well. As soon as the key was replaced, the other instruments became free. The operation of the control instrument required the co-operation of the signalmen at each end of the section. The ringing key of the train token instrument had to be held down, releasing the slides on the control instrument, which in turn released the occupation key. These slides were locked in a pulled-out position until the key was replaced in its lock. The signalman then pushed the slides in and the train token instrument was checked to make sure it was in working order.

Lever Collars

These were first introduced following the accident at Norton Fitzwarren on the GWR in 1890. although not all companies made their use obligatory. They vary in design according to the company, but their function is the same, that of immobilising the catch, and preventing the lever being moved. Each signal lever has a number and designation plate, the latter situated behind the lever frame. They are usually made of brass or cast iron.

Train Describers

These were introduced at busy junctions where it was necessary to describe both the train and its destination, and the number of beats needed became too complicated for the exchange of block signals. The system consists of a sending and receiving instrument operated by means of clockwork. The sending instrument has a needle which is stopped in any position by inserting a peg in the hole against the particular indication required. Tyers, Sykes and Westinghouse Brake & Saxby Signal Co were all makers of these instruments.

Single Line Working

The operation of single lines has produced many items for the collector. Prior to 1878 they were controlled by wooden staffs and tickets. In that year Edward Tyer patented an 'improved means and Apparatus for securing safety of traffic on single lines of railway . . . to secure the safety obtained by the staff system of working, and effect this by a combination of arrangements for the use of the staff or an equivalent for the staff, with means of electrically controlling its use.'

Instruments in adjacent signal boxes were electrically connected which allowed the signalmen to remove and issue to the driver of a train, one tablet. The driver with the tablet in his possession could then proceed to the end of the section, where it was handed to the signalman who replaced it in his instrument. This method is still in use, but there were many modifications and improvements of instruments to aid working.

The original Tyer patent took the form of two separate instruments, a receiver and a sender for the tablets. This was soon modified to what is known as the No 1 which was first installed on the Callender and Oban section of the Caledonian Railway. The tablets were the largest in diameter at just under 5½in. The tablet instruments Numbers 1, 2, 3, 4, and 6 were all similar

Single line signalling: inside the signal box the staff instrument can be seen silhouetted, whilst the signalman and locomotive fireman exchange staffs for the next section. The signal at clear indicates that the train can proceed to the next box.

A Great Western staff ticket. P. B. Whitehouse Collection.

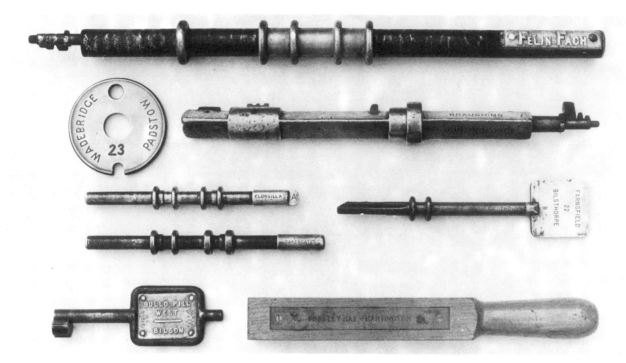

The main types of single line token. From top: Webb & Thompson staff–Aberayron-Felin Fach–with Annett key for an intermediate siding; Tyer No 6 tablet–Wadebridge-Padstow–as used on the LSWR; staff–Braughing-Buntingford–used in conjunction with metal tickets on GER; Webb & Thompson miniature staffs made by the Railway Signal Co, type 'S' Clonsilla-Drumree and type 'M' Hadley Junction-Oakengates; Railway Signal Co key token introduced in the 1920s–Farnsfield-Bilsthorpe; GWR key token introduced in 1914 to replace the large Webb & Thompson staff–Bullo Pill West-Bilson; British rail 'one engine in steam' staff–Parsley Hay-Hartington. F. B. Gell Collection.

in appearance and had the tablets in a column on top of one another. The tablets were withdrawn by means of a slide. The earlier instruments were non-returnable, that is the train had to pass through the section once the tablet had been issued and replaced in the instrument at the other end of the section. This was limiting where a train required to shunt in a section and wished to return to the same block post from whence it had come. The No 6 was the final development of this type, and was returnable.

The tablets for the number's 2, 3, 4, and 6, were just under 4½in. A pair of instruments usually had 30 tablets between them, except the No 5 which had only 24. The No 5 was probably made as a cheaper version. The tablets, just under 4in were held vertically in a circular rotating drum and removed from the instrument through a slot in the top. The final Tyer No 7 instrument was patented in 1898. The tablets were similar to that of the No 5 but the instrument was so arranged that the tablets were all used consecutively, by having two slides, one at the top to receive, the other at the bottom to withdraw. In later years the No 6 was the most widely adopted, and replaced many of the earlier types.

On certain lines where absolute block working was

not always required the original No 5 instrument was modified to form a permissive tablet instrument, known as No 5a and 5b. This enabled more than one train to proceed through the section, in the same direction, at one time. Such instruments are still in use in East Anglia.

In 1889 the train staff apparatus was invented by F. W. Webb and A. M. Thompson of the LNWR and this was to become Tyer's main competitor. This instrument worked on a similar principle to the tablet. A drum-shaped head containing the electrical mechanism was supported by a column containing a number of staffs, which were about 24in long. This method was used extensively on the GWR and LNWR. The Webb & Thompson staff often had a ground frame key at one end for unlocking the points at intermediate sidings, as had the earlier wooden staffs. The key was invented by James Edward Annett in 1875. The Tyer tablet could also be used at intermediate sidings where an appropriate tablet lock was provided. Later, the larger staff was improved by the Railway Signal Company who introduced the miniature staff, far easier to handle owing to its reduced size and weight.

The Tyer Company patented the key token instruments in 1912. It achieved the same object as a tablet or staff instrument, the main difference being the tokens which are keys, very suitable for controlling intermediate sidings. Initially made of iron, they were later in aluminium to reduce their weight. They were first adopted by the GWR in 1914 and gradually replaced many of the large Webb & Thompson staff instruments. There were a number of technical improvements over the years and British Railways are still installing them on many lines. The latest type being known as the 12a, with tokens made of an alloy.

In 1923 the Railway Signal Company developed a new key token instrument. This was very like a Yale door key, and considered a further improvement as it made the use of counterfeit tokens almost impossible. It was widely used on the LMS. When there are more trains in one direction than another there is a gradual accumulation of tokens at one end of the section. It is therefore necessary for the lineman to transfer a number of tokens back to the other instrument. To enable this to be done the various instruments were modified to hold a balancing magazine or carrier.

Staffs, tablets and key tokens had different configurations to prevent them being inserted in the wrong instrument. Basically tablets had three configurations A, B and C representing the different cut-outs. Key tokens had four, as did large Webb & Thompson staffs. Miniature staffs had six configurations by the different placings of metal collars on the staff. Configurations in general were known as A B C D and colours were Red Blue Green and Yellow respectively. Types E and F in the miniature staff were coloured Brown and Grey, and all had the appropriate section names on them.

To facilitate handling by driver and signalman, tablets, key tokens and miniature staffs were carried in pouches, often made of leather with a large hoop to pass an arm through. As it was necessary to reduce the train speed to 10mph for the pick-up and set-down

of a token, a mechanised exchanger was soon invented. Whitaker's exchanger consisted of a ground mechanism and a slidable bar attached horizontally to the engine. Both Tyer and Manson had similar versions.

The GWR had its own method, not an exchanger in the strict sense, but an arrangement to speed up hand exchanging. It consisted of three posts, one with a curved projecting arm to receive, a lamp post with a strong light, and a third fitted with a cast iron socket for pick-up. This third post was also fitted with a light.

To allow more than one train to pass along the single line section in the same direction consecutively, the Train Staff and Ticket System was used. At such staff stations a series of specially printed tickets were provided and kept in a box locked with a spring lock. Each driver was shown the staff, and issued with a ticket which gave the authority needed to pass along the section. The last train through took the staff which was deposited at the other end, ready for movement in the other direction. However to maintain the space interval, ordinary block indicators connect the two signal boxes to show that there is a train in the section.

In 1886 B. D. Wise of the Belfast & County Down Railway patented his train staff and ticket system. The tickets for either direction are locked into each end of the staff and can only be released by a key kept by the station master for his end. The staffs were used on the Cavan & Leitrim and the Welsh Highland Railway.

Many short branch lines such as those to collieries or works used a 'One Engine in Steam' staff where only one staff for the section exists.

Apart from losses resulting from the line closures, many signal boxes are now being demolished because of the introduction of multiple aspect or robot signalling. It may well be that in a few years there will be more of the earlier equipment in the hands of collectors than in those of British Rail.

A Tyer tablet in use on the 3ft gauge Tralee and Dingle Railway in the West of Ireland. P. B. Whitehouse Collection.

Staff and ticket box for Buckley Junction to Old Buckley. The metal tickets are replaced in the small hinged door on the top. F. B. Gell Collection.

Luggage Labels

D. A. Bone

It is regrettable that Conan Doyle never wrote a Sherlock Holmes story entitled 'The Mystery of the Faded Luggage Label'. Holmes, that great detective and traveller in the high noon of steam railways, would surely have welcomed the opportunity to resolve a crime, making deductions from the flimsy evidence of labels adhering to a portmanteau. The present-day collector, however, has ample scope to investigate the subject. At the very outset there is the dual question of why and when were luggage labels introduced. What appears certain is that passenger's luggage was originally conveyed on the roofs of the railway carriages. Such outside articles were secured by stout leather straps reinforced by wire. In the late 1840s it is known that the LNWR employed a special grade or railway worker called a 'strapper', with responsibility for securing luggage and keeping the straps in sound oiled condition. Passengers were still able, at least in theory, to control the loading, unloading and transfer of their possessions on the carriage roof, just as they did in the preceding stage coach era.

Because in one sense luggage and passengers were not separated, labelling cases and trunks with an indication of destination station was thought unnecessary. Doubtless most passengers fixed their own primitive labels, but there is no evidence that company ones were generally provided in these earliest days of rail travel. The subjection of luggage to the weather and to the filth of smoke-filled tunnels probably precipitated the concept of the guards van or separate luggage van, and then the luggage label itself. Railway staff became responsible for spotting which articles had to be unloaded—and unloaded promptly—at intermediate stations. Labels, clear and unmistakably official, enabled luggage to be so arranged in the van that this task was made easy. 'Amateur' labels with obscure handwriting would have been worse than useless in poorly-lit vehicles.

The labelling of luggage was in the interests of the railways from another point of view. Some companies, in particular the LBSCR and the GNR (Ireland), applied very strictly their rules and regulations governing the maximum authorised weight of luggage per passenger. Articles were thus only permitted to be brought onto the departure platform if they bore the official company's luggage labels, affixed by a railway servant. If the vigilant ticket inspector or porter suspected the 'free' entitlement was being abused, the luggage of the guilty passenger was not labelled until it had been weighed and any excess charged. It is a little hard to imagine too rigid an interpretation of these rules at small country stations, but at one time the fixing of an official label was essential before luggage could proceed.

Research into the vexed question of the oldest extant luggage label must necessarily be inconclusive. It is claimed for instance that a London and Greenwich Railway label lingers on, secure for all time on the lower portion of an antique chair! Broad conclusions can be drawn from facts such as the existence of Somerset Central Railway labels. That company operated from 1854–1862. Right over on the other side

A group of route labels with colour coding and other symbols. D. A. Bone Collection.

A group of parcel labels and a striking 'eggs' label issued by the Midland Railway. D. A. Bone Collection.

S.D.R.

Passenger Luggage.

Lidford to
Exeter

96

Great North of Scotland Railway.

LUGGAGE.

ROTHIEMAY

From .... *Elgin*

(A 425)

THE HIGHLAND RAILWAY.

LUGGAGE.

From **BLAIRATHOLL**
To London, St. Pancras
Via DUNKELD, FORTH BRIDGE, WAVERLEY, and MID.

C.V.R.

SUDBURY.

LUGGAGE.

Labels on which the word 'luggage' was actually printed: South Devon Railway; Great North of Scotland Railway; Highland Railway; Colne Valley Railway. D. A. Bone Collection.

of England, the North Eastern Railway took shape in 1854 with the amalgamation of the York, Newcastle and Berwick, York and North Midland, Leeds Northern and Malton and Driffield. NER labels are quite common, from a collector's point of view, but no label is thought to survive from its four constituents.

Railway activities in Sussex in the early and mid-1860s support the premise that it was during this particular period that labels came into general use. LBSCR labels 'New Arundel to Bramber' and 'Littlehampton Har. to Bramber' are relevant, and merit a moment's delving into history. Arundel and Littlehampton were both originally served by a station at Lyminster, on the LBSCR 'West Coast' Line, this station being opened in 1846. When the present Arundel station was opened in 1863, it was distinguished from Lyminster and from another 'Arundel' station (alias Ford Junction), by being named New Arundel. A station at Littlehampton was also opened in the period under discussion, but this initially carried the name Littlehampton Harbour. A ferry service operated from there to Honfleur in northern France, starting in about 1863. As the importance of this ferry service declined, the station name became plain Littlehampton. It seems probable that both these labels were printed not later than the mid-1860s.

It should be pointed out that comparatively few labels incorporate as part of the actual printing, the word 'luggage' itself. Certainly of the four post-grouping giants, only the LNER made much use of this rather obvious word. Two of the forerunners of the GWR in the South West, the Cornwall Railway and the South Devon Railway used the term 'Passenger's Luggage' (or Passenger Luggage) on some of their labels. Very early GWR labels did the same. Two Scottish Companies, the GNSR and the Highland, found it worthwhile to include the one word 'Luggage' on most of their labels, as did the diminutive Colne Valley Railway in East Anglia. In general, however, luggage labels confine themselves to imparting all, or some of the following information: Company name (in full or initials); Destination Station; Forwarding Station; Route, with 'To and From' as required. Date of printing is an occasional extra, as is a company's reference or code number, the number of labels printed in the batch, and the initials of the printing firm involved. An M&GN label 'To Worcester (Mid)' thus shows in small print: '(18)-V20-10,000 7-09 W&S Ltd' indicating label reference, order, number in batch, date of printing, and printer's initials.

Some companies, whether large or small, were intensely proud of their title, or so it seems from the fact that they had it printed in full on their labels. The LBSCR, for example, never economised by using any abbreviated version. The Caledonian also scorned

CALEDONIAN RAILWAY.

BRIGHTON, L.B.&S.C.

FROM

ABERDEEN

CAMBRIAN RAILWAYS.

TO

MERTHYR

(B. & M.)

244

C.R.

Bodmin Road to

Liverpool

Via Didcot

G. S. & W. R.

TO

WINCHESTER

Via FISHGUARD.

Glasgow & South Western Railway.

PAISLEY, CANAL

Labels issued by companies who shared the same initials but which caused no confusion: CR = Caledonian, Cornwall and Cambrian; GSWR = Glasgow & South Western and Great Southern & Western (Ireland). D. A. Bone Collection.

anything except its full name. This at least means the collector of today can hardly get 'Caledonian' confused with Cornwall Railway labels. The latter merely printed CR. Cambrian Railways labels also bear the full title. This company is unique, as far as the United Kingdom is concerned, in adopting the plural Railways. Another theoretical source of confusion could involve the Metropolitan Railway and the Midland Railway, but only the Metropolitan regularly used the initials 'MR' on their labels. Although confusion between Scottish and Irish Companies is unlikely, it is a coincidence that the Glasgow and South Western Rly and the Great Southern and Western Railway have initials in common, only the position of the 'and' is different. The Scottish company used its full title, whilst the Irish was generally content with GSWR.

In the 'abbreviations' category will be found the bulk of labels issued by the GWR, GER, Barry, LNWR, LC&DR, North Staffordshire, GNR (Ireland), MR (NCC), and GSWR. The company's name in full, or at least a version significantly greater than the bare

initials, was the practice of the LSWR, Glasgow & South Western, GNR, M&SWJR, Taff Vale, Rhymney, Midland, North London and LBSCR. The only company without a consistent policy on this point appears to be the NER. In this consideration of style used, the SECR practice is noteworthy. Their standard labels bear no indication whatsoever of company name. Some Irish labels, possibly early B&NCR, are also anonymous, as are some of the first label printings of the GER for ex-Eastern Counties Railway stations.

Before considering the main types of label once in common use, some thought should be given to how they were housed at stations. As all collectors know, certain labels are easy to come by, whilst others are rare. There are many reasons for this, but inadequate or exposed storage is one explanation. Labels with adhesive backs are obviously particularly vulnerable to damp, and GCR labels are certainly both rare and adhesively backed!

Perhaps the massive wooden tallboys, consisting of tiers of drawers each with a specimen label stuck by the recessed drawer handle, were not so great in reality as one might wish to imagine. Southern Railway main line stations certainly possessed these structures. At smaller SR stations, labels along with other paperwork, were more likely to be found in the booking office area, in the drawers of cabinets. The GWR favoured wooden hanging cupboards fixed to walls, generally convenient to the location of a luggage weighing platform. On opening the double doors to these cupboards, a great number of pigeon-holed racks were revealed, each with a specimen label stuck to the outer face. The pleasure of discovering two such well-filled cupboards at an ex-GWR station as recently as 1971 need hardly be described. Smaller pigeon-holed cabinets, forming part of the general parcels office furniture, was the practice at other GWR stations. Other companies protected their labels by using cupboards with sliding doors. At the smaller LNER (ex-GER) stations, labels were housed horizontally, not vertically. A shallow box, divided inside into sections, rather like a ladies' sewing box, was provided with legs and given a lid. But modernisation of station premises has seen the end of such cupboards and cabinets and makes the collector's task increasingly daunting.

One elementary label classification is between those quoting despatching station, and those quoting both despatching and receiving stations. A company like the LBSCR, who believed in having a printed label from every station to every station on their system, must have had higher printing costs than the Midland who seldom strayed from the destination only style. Remembering that labels were designed to ensure safe arrival of a piece of luggage, their printing for very short distance transits now appears something of an extravagance. The Metropolitan Railway 'Paddington (Bishops Road) to Edgware Road' must surely get the reward for the shortest possible distance. The LBSCR can contribute two runners-up, 'Purley Oaks to Selhurst' and 'East Croydon to Crystal Palace', distances of 3 and $2\frac{3}{4}$ miles respectively. The GWR's best could be 'Stonehouse to Brimscombe', being $5\frac{1}{2}$ miles. The GWR employed place-to-place labels up to the mid-1880s, thereafter destination only was the rule, apart from labels specially printed for Irish or Isle of Man transits. Companies who made fair use of the 'place-to-place' type include the Taff Vale, GNSR, Caledonian, Cornwall, Metropolitan, Met.&GC Joint, and L&Y. The SR followed LSWR practice and did not adopt the broadbrush place-to-place approach of the LBSCR, but had an extensive 'Waterloo to . . .' series. LSWR included destinations on the M&SWJ Rly, so that very improbable labels such as Waterloo to Withington, Cerney and Ashton Keynes, and Rushey Platt exist. The same series includes stations on the S&D. One 'place-to-place' which deserves inclusion is a

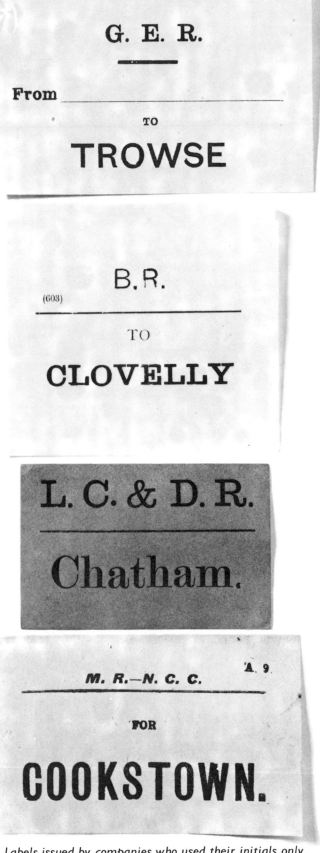

Labels issued by companies who used their initials only. D. A. Bone Collection.

London and South Western Ry.

787

FROM WATERLOO TO
WITHINGTON
(Via ANDOVER JUNCTION)

Midland and South Western Junction Railway.

(170)   [W. & S. Ltd.]

TO
BRISTOL

473
Great Northern Railway.
TO
DOUGLAS
ISLE OF MAN, VIA LIVERPOOL.

(70)

Rhymney Railway.

DOWLAIS

London Brighton & South Coast Railway.

Horeham Road to
Anerley

Labels issued by companies who gave their names in full: London and South Western; Midland and South Western Junction; Rhymney; London Brighton & South Coast; Great Northern. D. A. Bone Collection.

specimen where the transit detail of 'Ettington to Cheltenham' is swamped by the impressive name of the companies of origin, 'East and West Junction and Stratford-on-Avon Towcester and Midland Junction Railways'.

Many other examples could be produced of 'place-to-place' labels covering transits not merely within the system of the despatching company, but throughout the British Isles. If 'Paddington (Bishops Road) to Edgware Road' is accepted as one of the shortest distances possible, a Caledonian 'Aberdeen to Brighton' could be one of the longest. 'Bodmin Road to Liverpool via Didcot', the message on a Cornwall Railway label, would also have involved quite a mileage, in a roundabout way! No label collector can ever feel his collection is complete, against the background of all the 'to and from' combinations possible.

Labels were vital to ensure luggage was off-loaded promptly at the correct intermediate station of junction. It was necessary therefore, when the journey was lengthy, for the approved route and significant transhipment points to be known. Through trains, or through carriages, were a great feature in the halcyon days of the railways, but even then much luggage could expect to change trains several times on a cross-country journey. The mandatory route was either quoted in the body of the label, or was supplied by the

use of a separate 'route label'. Such special labels were used on parcels, packages, and on 'luggage in advance' items, more perhaps than on ordinary accompanied cases and trunks. As a means of ensuring quick identification, a route label would fail dismally if it were indistinct. In practice many of these labels relied on bright colours, or a bold symbol, to attract attention and to remind handling staff of the official transit pattern. Use of route labels varies between companies, or perhaps it would be fairer to say that few route labels issued by some companies have apparently survived. The GWR issued a considerable number, nearly all long and thin, and on coloured paper. A broad division can be made between those quoting one significant station only, such as 'Via Banbury' and those involving Paddington, such as 'Paddington . . . for transfer to LNER (GE Section)'. Somerset and Dorset route labels (post Grouping) were on pale blue paper. GER route labels, and GER style ones issued by the LNER, were not only often on distinctive blue or pink paper, but additionally incorporated a symbol. To recognise one of these symbols—'X', an inverted 'V', ' \ ' are typical—on a label of a particular bold colour, would instantly explain the handling treatment needed. The LNER soon abandoned the GER symbol system and made more use of special labels, sometimes printed on bright shades of paper, and covering place-to-place transits. Neatly printed, these were of pleasing design and incorporate route detail plus a two-letter identification code enclosed in a circle. A typical example would be 'Aberdeen to Skipton via Bridges, Carlisle, Settle and L.M.S. (CA) '. The GER also used a similar two-letter code on some of their route labels.

Labels which combined destination station, with an unmistakable colour clue to routing were employed by the LBSCR for Isle of Wight transits. A bold diagonal red cross, from corner to corner, was the feature. After the grouping, this particular means of identification was continued on a range of SR labels for a while, before a blue upright cross marking became standard. By contrast LSWR labels for destinations on the Isle of Wight differed little from their standard type, although some were printed on pale mauve paper. There was however a LSWR route label series, including ones appropriate to the Isle of Wight. LMSR route labels were generally plain–black print on white paper– merely spelling out the required route such as 'Via Worcester and GW'. In this context the LMS adopted the Midland Railway style. The LNWR did not apparently find much need for route labels.

The way in which a newly-formed company adopted the habits of one particular constituent is an interesting sidelight on the battles for power that followed an amalgamation. Old customs die hard, and three generations of route label may exist for one pattern of transit. A GWR example quoting 'Via Great Western + LSW Railways', became replaced by 'For Transfer to Southern Rly (L + SW Section)', and finally by an early BR 'For Transfer to Southern Region (L + SW Section)'. All bear the same GWR form code no. 4642. The SR became rather confused in the very early days of its existence. It adopted the LSWR style of ordinary luggage label and route label, but somehow a SR route label quoting 'To Midland Rly' was printed! The LNER also allowed a label howler to be printed with 'Via Peterboro' and Midland'. An intense reluctance to depart from old styles and names was no doubt the reason for some early LMS labels to be practically identical to 'Caledonian' or 'Highland' ones. Very similar styles of printing, colour and layout were followed, the labels quoting 'Caledonian Section' and 'Highland Section' of the LMS respectively.

It took some years before the LMS seemed able to standardise its labels. When it did, it had the code E.R.O: 21556 as part of the printing identification number. In the early days of the LNER, some labels very similar to GNSR types were printed for that distant section of the company, but the LNER adopted the GER label style eventually, but often adding 'to, from and route' detail.

To censure the printer for label mistakes is a little unkind, bearing in mind the minute percentage of error

An 'anonymous' label issued by the South Eastern and Chatham Railway. D. A. Bone Collection.

that has been traced. The task of keeping all the racks at thousands of stations well stocked, must have involved quite a measure of planning and office organisation. The printing of labels, with other railway paperwork, appears to have been done partly by the companies' own printing departments, and partly by the commercial trade. Most collections of labels will be found to contain specimens showing in small type, the printer's initials and the order number. These jumbles of letters and figures should not be confused with the railway companies' own form number. Midland Railway passenger forms (including labels) bear a 'P F' no., and goods forms 'GF'. Nearly all SR labels bear a reference 'Stock/787'. The M&GN label quoted earlier 'To Worcester (Mid)' includes 'W&SLtd' in the small detail, standing for the printers, Waterlow & Sons. Other M&GN labels, as well as some GNR ones, bear the printers' initials 'H.C. Ltd', or 'H.C. & G. Ltd'.

Waterlows handled printing requirements for nearly all the pre-grouping companies. This association with the railways may stem from the fact that Sir Sidney Waterlow, the son of the founder, was a director of the LC&DR. In their time Waterlows have printed tens of millions of labels, tickets and other railway forms. They did not have the monopoly, for Bemrose (who handled much LMS printing in the 1930s), Harrisons, and McCorquodales were also responsible for large quantities. Irish printers included Carswell & Sons Ltd. The great variation in printing styles, with NER labels for instance, suggests quite a number of labels were probably printed by small local concerns. Railway documents with printers' names like 'Sentinel Derry' and 'Quinnell and Sons, Tralee', exist and it seems reasonable to assume that local jobbing printers were responsible for the labels as well.

As we have seen, a luggage label can carry a variety of information ranging from a single word on a typical GER, to a whole paragraph on some LNER examples. Some companies were extravagant in their use of un-

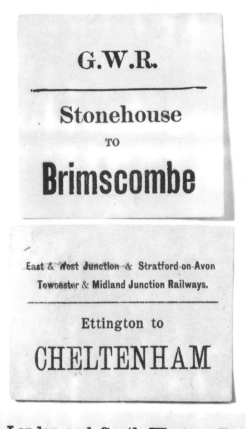

East & West Junction & Stratford-on-Avon
Towcester & Midland Junction Railways.

Ettington to

CHELTENHAM

London and South Western Ry.
787
From WATERLOO
TO

Cerney & Ashton Keynes
VIA ANDOVER

London Brighton & South Coast Railway.

Purley Oaks to

Selhurst

A group of 'place to place' labels. D. A. Bone Collection.

necessary words. A NER label using three words where two would certainly be enough is 'Castle Eden Station'. The chance of a separate and confusable Castle Eden halt, crossing or platform, at which luggage could be unloaded seems remote! Nevertheless whilst the inclusion of the word 'Station' achieves nothing except a measure of uniqueness, the destination place name on a label might not necessarily be a railway station. In the range of standard style labels issued by the Southern Railway, are two quoting very

different non-passenger station destinations, 'Stewarts Lane' and 'Totland Bay'. Barry Railway is represented by a 'To Clovelly' which presumably involved steamer via Barry Pier. A specimen from the Caledonian Rly, would seem to fall into the same category, 'Loch Tay via Killin Pier from Edinburgh Princes Street'. This label is, however, something of a red herring. Loch Tay was the name of an actual railway station, on the very banks of the loch. This station is referred to by a note in the appropriate table of a 1922 Bradshaw as 'Killin Pier'. Perhaps the label should have read 'Loch Tay (Killin Pier)'.

Parcel labels are similar in appearance to luggage labels. They were used in circumstances where small consignments, clearly not falling into the freight side of railway operations, travelled by passenger train. Examination of these specially printed and distinctive labels in the GWR's range, strongly suggest that the transits catered for were from 'country to town' and not vice versa. 'Blank' parcel labels with spaces for the completion of the 'To' and 'From' and 'Route via' entries were also available. Three quite typical GWR parcel labels are from Suckley to Coventry, Leeds and Liverpool. These were probably mainly used in connection with the heavy seasonal traffic in soft fruit, apples, pears etc, which the Suckley area on the Worcestershire/Herefordshire border produces in good measure. Parcel labels existed pre-grouping, as a GWR 'South Molton to Brighton LBSCR' proves. As with luggage labels, the total of all the different 'To and From' parcel labels printed defies accurate assessment. Other companies may have preferred to print labels with just the despatching station detail, if two LNWR 'Parcel from Pontsarn (for Vaynor)' are typical. These latter two illustrate the distinction between labels bearing the message 'Paid' and those with the more ominous 'To Pay'.

The method behind the use of parcel labels, as far as the GWR was concerned, was very broadly as follows. If a farmer or trader regularly sent scores of boxes of fruit, mushrooms, flowers etc to a city market, he would have a ledger account with the company. A label in the 'Carriage Paid' series would be fixed to each of his packages. If the carriage charge was payable at some later stage, or by some other party, a label with a 'Total to Pay' entry was used. The 'Carriage Paid' labels bore reference No. 135a. In general the 'Total to Pay' labels had GWR Form No. 135.

Luggage, route and parcel labels more often than not record a station now demolished, or a route long since abandoned. A particularly uncommon label thus becomes the excuse for a mild bout of nostalgia or an exercise in detection. No different to hundreds of other GWR luggage labels of the basic type, is one with the destination 'Kingsbridge Road'. Already this may have

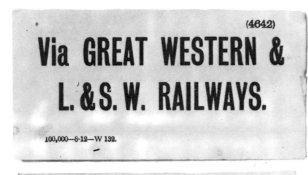

Via GREAT WESTERN &
L.&S.W. RAILWAYS.

(4642)

100,000—8-12—W 132.

FOR TRANSFER TO

SOUTHERN REGION

(4642)

(L. & S.W. Section)

Via_____

25,000—Est. 475—5/30. S

(4642)

FOR TRANSFER TO

SOUTHERN RAILWAY

(L. & S.W. Section)

Via_____

SOUTHERN RAILWAY.

(15/33)

Stock
(843)

To MIDLAND Ry.

via................................

A group of labels for luggage in transit between different companies. D. A. Bone Collection.

of the short lived 'City to City' service, basically London (Broad Street) to Birmingham (New Street) which was introduced in 1908/1909. The NLR was by then virtually part of the LNWR, and the latter were disturbed by the popularity of the GWR's two-hour Birmingham expresses, using the new shorter route via Bicester. So a rival express was supplied to tempt city businessmen. About $2\frac{1}{4}$ hours was needed for the journey. Trains called at Coventry, and some continued through to Wolverhampton–hence the NLR label.

A final word of warning should be added for the uninitiated collector. Just as banknotes have been forged, examples of forged luggage labels are also known. The time and effort in producing a passable imitation of the real thing, would seem out of all proportion to any gain by the forger! He could have one of three aims, firstly the addition to his collection of a rarity, secondly the exchange of the bogus label for some genuine rarity, or thirdly the desire to fool the experts and puzzle fellow collectors. A Southern Railway 'Waterloo to Lower Norwood via Clapham Junction' appears to fall into this third category. The label looks genuine, but as far as can be determined, no Lower Norwood station has ever existed.

The study of luggage labels can be an amusing and stimulating hobby, but the prospective collector will not nowadays find the establishment of a collection an easy task. More than a quarter of a century has elapsed since nationalisation, and the chance discovery of SR, GWR, LNER, or LMS labels at existing stations is now remote. A courteous enquiry is rarely frowned upon by BR staff, but 'expect nothing' should be the attitude. Comfort may be taken from the fact that the writer obtained LBSCR and GER items from a London suburban station only in 1973. A scrutiny of the monthly railway magazines will sometimes reveal in the classified advertisement column sellers of miscellaneous printed matter including labels. Membership of a preservation society or transport club can be a useful means of obtaining or exchanging paper relics and at a 'Steam Open Day' oddments can sometimes be bought for nominal sums.

conjured up a picture of a Dublin station, especially since the GWR did print standard labels to Irish destinations. But the collector's research will show Kingsbridge Road was the name of the Devonshire station, later known as Wrangaton. Before the Brent to Kingsbridge branch was opened in 1893, Kingsbridge Road was the nearest station for Kingsbridge itself. A further instance of a label providing incentive for a line of research, could be found in a North London Railway 'Wolverhampton'. The NLR had a curiously suburban flavour about it, and 'Wolverhampton' seems altogether too remote. That label, however, is a reminder

SOUTHERN RAILWAY.

(1/24)

787

FROM WATERLOO TO

LOWER NORWOOD

(Via Clapham Junc.)

A warning to collectors. This is apparently a regular SR label, but there is no such station as Lower Norwood! D. A. Bone Collection.

Posters and Handbills

Maurice Rickards

The era of the railway is the era of communications. The first half of the 19th century saw not only the first public passenger line with steam, the Stockton and Darlington, but the coming of the electric telegraph, the inception of a full-scale postal service and the mechanisation of print production.

Considered separately, each development was crucial. Collectively their impact was overwhelming. Each reinforced the other; each was supported by the other. The printed image loomed as large on the railway as anywhere. Perhaps larger. With an apparently boundless captive audience, and with an endless flow of invitations, warnings and injunctions, the railway generated posters and notices from the start. Historically the poster is an ingredient as native to the railway concept as the train itself. We see it most poignantly in its absence. The derelict station of the 1970s is more than merely disused; it lacks not only hardware, not only equipment and rolling stock, but 'décor'. Without its complement of advertisement and admonition, the railway scene is bleak indeed.

The railway companies were quick to exploit the attention-value of their walls and notice-boards and they made no bones about their message. They spoke in the clearest terms in the heaviest of black type: *The Directors are determined, by every means in their power, to detect any Party attempting to Defraud the Company and have the offenders visited with the severest Punishments . . . .* Thus the Newcastle and Carlisle Railway Company in 1847. It must be said that notices directed to passengers were sometimes indistinguishable in tone from those directed to staff.

But cheek-by-jowl with admonition was seduction. The passenger, whatever his transgressions, had also to be encouraged; in the same format, and in the same daunting typefaces, he was fairly wooed: *The Wonder of 1851! From York to London and back for a Crown,* says a Midland Railway announcement for the Great Exhibition, adding for good measure that the Company also provides 'Tickets of Reference for Approved Lodgings' for those who venture the journey unprepared with hotel bookings. A further encouragement appears in a paragraph on the matter of risk: *The Managers have much pleasure in stating that the immense numbers who have travelled under their arrangements have been conducted in perfect safety—indeed in the history of the Midland Lines, no accident, attended with personal injury, has ever happened to an Excursion Train . . . .*

It was in the department of seduction that the railway poster was finally to flourish. As passengers and staff were slowly tamed (though neither group was ever to rise wholly above suspicion) the companies began to concentrate on blandishment.

With the development of new reproduction techniques the typographic invitation gave way to pictures; black and white gave way to colour. By the early years of the new century, the term 'railway poster' had acquired distinct connotations: full colour lithographs; splendid scenery; Art for Railways' Sake. Some of the productions were considered good enough to put up (minus their lettering) as decorations in railway waiting rooms.

AYLESBURY RAILWAY.

FIVE POUNDS REWARD.

Some evil-disposed Person or Persons have lately *feloniously Stolen and carried away*, a quantity of **RAILS, STAKES,** and **MATERIALS,** belonging to the Company, for which any Offender, on Conviction, is liable to Transportation for Seven Years.

Several **STAKES** driven into the Ground for the purpose of setting out the Line of Railway, *have also been Pulled up and Removed,* by which a Penalty of Five Pounds for each Offence has been incurred, half Payable to the Informer and half to the Company.

The above Reward will be paid on Conviction, in addition to the Penalty, to any Person who will give Evidence sufficient to Convict any Offender guilty of either of the above Crimes, on application to Mr. **HATTEN** or Mr. **ACTON TINDAL,** of Aylesbury.

By Order of the Directors.

Aylesbury, August 18th, 1838.

May, Printer, Aylesbury.

Aylesbury handbill for 1838. National Railway Museum.

LOST

On the Rail Road between Preston and Birmingham, on Friday, 9th of September,

A LARGE
PORTMANTEAU,

of Black Leather, with a Painted Cover, marked in white letters "*G. Puzzi*," and on the Portmanteau itself a Brass Plate engraved "*G. Puzzi*," containing a white leather Portfolio, with Trinkets and Jewellery, and a variety of Papers; also a large quantity of Wearing Apparel and Linen marked with the initials "G. P." Also the amount of 150 New Sovereigns, and a quantity of Silver, the amount not exactly known. Among the Trinkets was a large Gold Seal, marked with a double " P."

Whoever will give information of the above loss to Mr. WALTER, 56, Davies Street, Berkeley Square, London, that will lead to the recovery of the Property---or if Stolen, the conviction of the Offender or Offenders---shall be most handsomely Rewarded.

Septr. 15, 1842.   London : Wm. Davy, Printer, Gilbert-st., Oxford-st

Passenger's announcement for 1842. National Railway Museum.

In the historical perspective of print technology the black and white typographic announcement belongs broadly to the 19th century; colour is the hallmark of the 1900s. For many collectors they form two distinct specialisations. Because of its technical simplicity the typographic announcement lends itself most readily to 20th-century reproduction for collectors. Single colour working (mostly black) and undemanding detail allow anyone with a small litho printing press to turn out passable facsimiles of the genuine article. All that is needed is photographic access to the original.

There is no question of producing 'counterfeits'; the printed result is instantly recognisable, even by the layman, as a modern reproduction. Paper quality and printing characteristics are far remote from the real thing. But for those whose interest is in the poster's content rather than its pedigree the facsimile is a valid collector's item.

It is after all in its wording and layout that the typographic poster makes its greatest appeal. In its phraseology, its technical references and its evocations of

bygone social conditions the black and white announcement can often convey atmosphere more graphically than its full-colour counterpart. And whereas the genuine article has become a rarity, the reproduction has the merit of being not merely available but well within the reach of the ordinary collector.

Most collections—photocopies, reproductions or originals—are presented in historical sequence by subject or geographical area. Categories may include line-openings, warnings, reward notices, station name-changes, timetable and fare adjustments and excursions. (A demonstration in favour of Garibaldi was the subject of one York–to–London excursion in the 1860s.)

Closely allied to the black and white typographical poster is the handbill—often a miniature poster in itself—giving details of fares and special services. These, in turn derived from the canal and coach leaflet of earlier times, were later printed with an element of colour, often appearing as a single-colour printing on coloured paper.

With an adroit admixture of typographic poster and handbill it is possible to convey a coherent narrative of early railway development without further comment

CHEAP TRAIN.

Wrestling Match

BETWEEN

IVISON, OF CARLISLE, AND

JAMESON, OF NEWCASTLE, AT

HAYDON BRIDGE

On TUESDAY, July 29, 1845.

The Public are respectfully informed, that the **Directors of the Newcastle and Carlisle Railway Company** have kindly consented to an application to convey Passengers **FROM NEWCASTLE** (and all Intermediate Stations) **TO HAYDON BRIDGE** and back, for

One Fare,

By the Train which leaves the Newcastle Station at 7 o'clock in the Morning of the above day---to return by the Trains in the Evening.

Newcastle, July 16, 1845.

Printed by W. DOUGLAS, Observer Office, High Street, Gateshead.

Newcastle & Carlisle handbill for 1845.
National Railway Museum.

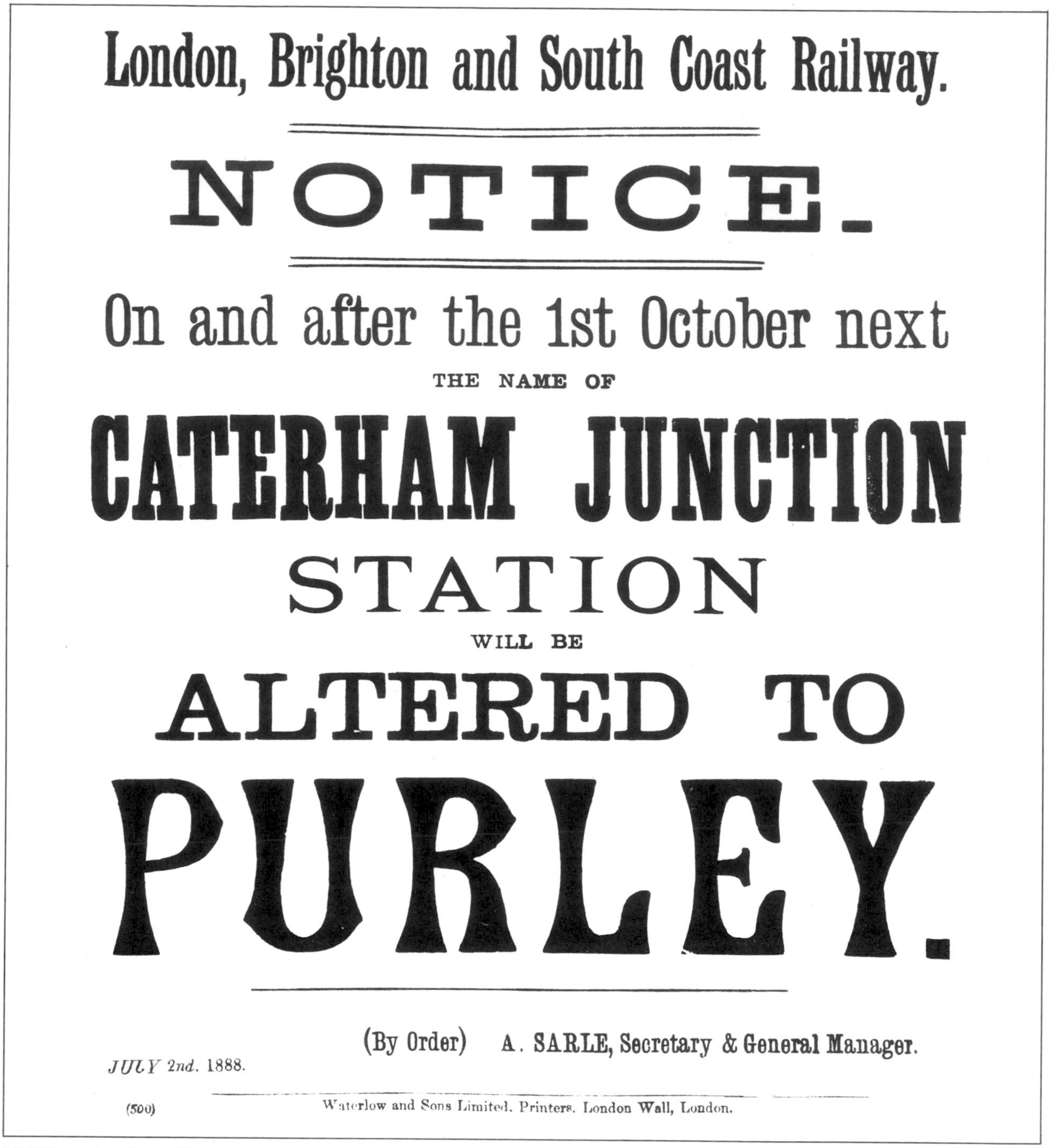

London, Brighton and South Coast Railway.

NOTICE.

On and after the 1st October next

THE NAME OF

CATERHAM JUNCTION

STATION

WILL BE

ALTERED TO

PURLEY.

(By Order)   A. SARLE, Secretary & General Manager.

JULY 2nd. 1888.

(500)   Waterlow and Sons Limited. Printers. London Wall, London.

LBSCR notice for 1888.
National Railway Museum.

or captioning. Some collectors concentrate on the 'overlap' period, in which coach, canal and railway struggled for supremacy. Others confine their interest to particular aspects of development. One specialist deals only with 'internal' posters–notices relative to staff regulations, terms of employment, strike announcements etc; another collects items of railway controversy–announcements of 'No-Trains-on-Sundays' campaigns and protests against proposed new lines. In each case the collection is arranged in chronological sequence, telling the story as it happened.

For the collector who admits photocopies and reproductions conservation problems hardly arise. For the 'originals-only' man, however, there are difficulties. Unlike the rag paper of the early 1800s, the late Victorian product tends to become brittle with age. Even with careful handling some of the later notices may disintegrate at a touch.

A collection of printed notices need not necessarily confine itself to items of great age. To the railway historian of the future today's announcement may be of

GNR poster by John Hassall.

SR poster by Austin Cooper.

engrossing interest. Among contemporary specimens in one collection is a BR Southern Region announcement declaring that 'British Rail regret inconvenience caused by any action taken by ASLEF train drivers and emphasise that any disruption is in no way the responsibility of NUR train drivers or other uniformed staff'. Another example is the Waterloo Station appeal to passengers not to feed the station pigeons, which 'as many passengers know to their cost' cause a nuisance. Announcements of this kind, though sidelights on the railway scene, are tomorrow's museum exhibits.

Rewarding as the study of the typographic poster may be, for most people the true railway poster is the colour-pictorial. This is the very epitome of the railways' golden age. It has been collected, not only in recent times as a nostalgia-object, but almost from its inception as an inexpensive objet d'art.

Some colour-pictorials were undoubtedly better than others. Some, like Hassall's leaping fisherman, had no pretensions to art; some were merely pretty; others were just pictorial railwayana. But most – particularly those that had a long 'run' – became much-loved features of the railway world; they acquired the same comforting familiarity as the enamel 'Virol' signs and the Nestlé slot machines.

The Hassall opus first appeared in 1908. Though it is not a work of art, it is clearly a first-class poster. In its simplicity, good humour and memorability it incorporates all the essentials of poster impact. It achieved worldwide fame and is regarded by many as the classic railway poster. But it created no new railway poster style. Like Alfred Leete's pointing Kitchener of World War I, it was a one-off wonder. It set no new standards, evoked no copyists. But it is among the world's most durable designs. The poster has been reprinted, adapted, redrawn and re-published innumerable times. The fisherman motif has been incorporated in the Skegness mayoral chain of office, and at Hassall's funeral in 1948 Skegness sent a floral tribute in the shape of a leaping fisherman. The artist's fee for the design, forty years earlier, had been £12. (The Great Northern Railway had paid the bill.)

The resort/railway double-act became standard promotional practice. As the seaside holiday idea caught on, the railway companies cashed in. Soon the companies were selling not railways but places. In some cases, not to miss a trick, railway company directors invested in the resorts they served; here again, one historical development fed another: rail business was resort business.

On the whole the pictorial railway poster was a long time getting off the ground. Colour lithography, widely available since the turn of the century, had brought only indifferent railway designs. Apart from Hassall's £12-worth, little of major importance was to appear until the early 1920s, when the LMS turned, for a change, to the 'fine' artist.

With the advent of artists like Norman Wilkinson, (who had designed several striking steamship posters for the LNWR), Fred Taylor and Frank Mason, the railway poster found status and respectability. By the mid-twenties there were few academic painters who had not at least been asked to produce a railway poster: Maurice Greiffenhagen, William Orpen, Frank Brangwyn – Royal Academicians became railway artists.

But the truth of it was that they did not really become poster artists. Their work, though specially commissioned, was for the most part 'gallery art', paintings in their normal studio style reproduced on the central area of a poster-size sheet of paper. In the margins left for the purpose above and below the picture, the Big Four printed place-names and their own names. Occasionally, as in the case of the Southern Railway, they ventured to add such vital information as 'H. A. Walker, General Manager'.

These productions were not posters in the normally accepted sense of the word. They were outdoor wall decorations, admirably suited to the musings of the waiting passenger and closely akin to the London Transport 'decor' posters of today – good to look at, and devoid of all but the most rudimentary message.

By contrast, out in the wider world, the poster moved ahead. The later twenties and thirties brought true poster artists, men whose designs packed a selling punch. These designers, adept at the integration of word and image, were not merely artists; they were visual salesmen. Unlike the academicians, whose work was only marginally applicable to the market place, the new designers started their thinking in the market place itself. Austin Cooper, Cassandre, Tom Purvis, E. McKnight Kauffer, and later Pat Keely, F. H. K. Henrion, Hans Unger, Stan Krol and Abram Games – these men brought to the word 'poster' a new dynamic meaning.

Sooner or later – reluctantly at first, but with growing confidence – the railway companies took up with them; the railway poster had moved on on from the Rail Academy.

By the late thirties the scene had changed almost completely; with Purvis serving as a pictorial halfway house, and Cassandre and Cooper presenting a near-abstract ultimate, it appeared that the colour-pictorial was due for a long rest. In the late forties and fifties, when colour photography moved in, the impression was strengthened. The railways had seen the last of the oil-painting.

But not quite. Cuneo moved in, too.

Terence Cuneo, painter of warfare, heavy engineering and royalty, brought new life to the railway pictorial. He did so not only in his capacity as painter but

LMS poster by A. Mouron-Cassandre.

as a dedicated enthusiast: inverting the old formula, his poster-paintings focused not on destinations but on the railway itself.

In a superb series of canvases he expressed the drama, the power and the poetry, of steam – the fascination of the old-time railway tradition and the excitement and promise of the future. His paintings are classics. Original canvases are today worth very large sums; poster reproductions are virtually unobtainable. No other artist has conveyed the railway scene as graphically as Cuneo. Unlike the majority of painters, his artistic sense is matched by an intimate understanding of railway hardware. Most of his work was done on the spot often in difficult conditions, and his railway scenes are not merely magnificent, they are generally unassailably truthful.

The British Rail posters of today are not the pictorial pieces of even a decade back. If they are pictorial at all, they tend to use photographs to attract custom. Posters advertising motorail services, restaurant car services, mini weekends and 'See a Friend This Weekend' are unlikely to become rare collectors' items. There is a good reason for this change. In the old days when most people travelled by train, the pictorial poster was there to preach to the converted. It soft sold the delights of a summer resort for next year's holiday, or it showed

the straightness of a particular company's main line. Only in the 1930s did it have to persuade the traveller that speed, comfort and price were positive benefits. Today rail travel is 'Inter City' and commuter and more sophisticated promotion techniques are required. The wheel has almost come full circle, and railway advertising, including posters has once again become factual – hard economics do not allow for beguiling pictures with no return.

In the early years of the poster, at the turn of the century, enthusiasts used to creep out at night and peel off newly-posted Toulouse-Lautrecs and Chérets today the collector contents himself with less easy prey. For the railway poster fan it is the early Purvis, the vintage Austin Cooper, or the halcyon Cuneo. Soon these too may be making saleroom records.

Although pictorial posters may have disappeared from our main lines, some comfort may be drawn from the fact that the 'preserved' or tourist lines still commission them, and many of these are worthy of attention. (Both the Talyllyn and Dart Valley railways, for example, had Cuneos.) Such posters are inexpensive, and it is encouraging to think that collections may still be embarked upon with such characteristic examples.

Opposite page:
LNER poster by Tom Purvis.
BR poster by Terence Cuneo.

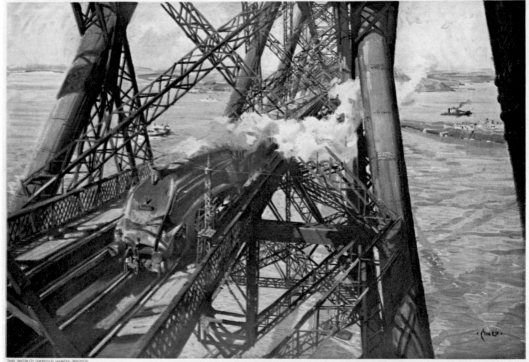

A group of glazed earthenware inkwells made for the Great Central, LNWR, LMS and Midland Railway. Cattell Collection.

A collection of railway china including examples made for the GCR, LNER, GWR, L&YR and Pullman. W. H. McAlpine Collection.

Cutlery, China and Glass

Rex Blaker

In an era when anything connected with railways is at a premium, from complete locomotives to luggage labels, it is strange that cutlery, china, and glass have been rather neglected by collectors. This is probably because the majority of enthusiasts are unaware of the extent of the railways' interest in the catering industry and, indeed, few railway historians have devoted much attention to the subject. Many collectors will be surprised to learn, therefore, that in the 1930s Britain's railways operated seventy-nine hotels and that this was the largest chain of hotels in the world at that time. It included some of the best-known in the country, such as the Midland at Manchester, the Queen's at Leeds, the Adelphi at Liverpool, and Gleneagles which has, of course, an international reputation.

In addition the railways provided a chain of refreshment rooms extending from Penzance in the extreme south to Dingwall and Elgin in the far north. The LMS alone ran over a hundred but, not content with that, they opened dining rooms at all major stations and at some quite small places such as Stirling and Bletchley. Many of these dining rooms dated back to the days before dining cars were introduced and trains would make special 'refreshment stops' at places like Carlisle for the convenience of long-distance passengers. The rooms, served by waiters or waitresses, provided meals of a standard comparable with those obtainable at most hotels but at considerably lower prices. Many of the regular customers were local residents who had no intention of travelling and who

had therefore to purchase a platform ticket before they could take advantage of the service offered!

Better known to most travellers were the several hundred dining car services which provided full meals in sumptuously furnished and luxuriously equipped rolling stock.

For the collector the important point is that every one of these establishments and trains was equipped down to the last detail and that all of the equipment was badged with the initials, or even the full coat of arms, of the owning company. The inventory is vast, ranging from huge punch-bowls and tea-urns to salt and mustard spoons. In between could be found everything else which might possibly be required in the kitchen or at the table—tankards, grape scissors, soup tureens, ladles, meat skewers, gravy boats, oyster and snail forks, wine funnels, vegetable dishes, finger bowls, toast racks, nutcrackers, cocktail shakers, lobster picks, ham stands, muffin dishes, pepper mills, asparagus dishes, cruet stands, and so on. Only the best was good enough for the railway catering services and the whole inventory was produced in quality silver-plate by such well-known manufacturers as Walker & Hall, Elkington, and Mappin & Webb. The china (even the chamber-pots, many of which were generously decorated and gilded) bore the famous trade marks of Minton and Spode.

Although most of the dining rooms were closed in the 1950s, and the list of hotels has grown shorter, substantial quantities of their equipment are still in use in the remaining cafeterias and bars. It is worthy

The LMS laurel wreath device adopted in 1925. This was used on silver plate, china and glass.

of the collector's attention and, unlike so many other railway relics, can be put to practical use in the home. The hobby can be extended to include an interest in the hotels themselves and in locating those which are now closed. For example the frontages of Lime Street and Exchange Stations in Liverpool were once the North Western and Exchange Hotels respectively and other semi-derelict buildings, as at Holyhead and Bletchley, may still be recognised as former hotels. Some remain open under new owners such as those at Crewe, Stoke-on-Trent, Dornoch, and Strathpeffer. Others, at Felixstowe, Preston, and Sidmouth, are today used as offices, and the recently-closed St Enoch Hotel in Glasgow awaits demolition and re-development. Any collector fortunate enough to find examples of cutlery from these hotels can congratulate himself on the possession of rare items.

Railway cutlery falls roughly into two categories. The more important is that which is badged with some kind of monogram, garter device, or, better still, a crest or coat of arms. The other variety is that which is more simply stamped with the initials of the owning company to which were sometimes added the further initials 'R.R.' for refreshment rooms, or 'R.D.' for refreshment department. Most cutlery of this latter type had a cheaper finish and was almost certainly either made specially for staff canteens or produced during the World Wars when nothing better could be obtained. It is not possible here to give a list of all the permutations and combinations which could be (and were) formed from different arrangements of various initials. Such a record would fill a book. All that can be

attempted here is to whet the would-be collector's appetite by giving him some idea of the range of items likely to be met in the course of his searches.

The London Midland & Scottish Railway and its constituents

The LMS was not only the largest of the four great railway companies but was also the largest hotel owner. It took over seventeen hotels in England and Wales and ten and two-thirds in Scotland (two-thirds because a third of the Station Hotel, Perth, belonged to the LNER). It also acquired four hotels in Northern Ireland to complete the largest hotel group in Europe at that time.

In the early days the LMS armorial device appeared on the cab sides of locomotives and almost everywhere else. It is not surprising, therefore, to find it on the company's silverware. It was also used on crockery where it appeared in blue on plain white china, sometimes with the initials of a former-owning company beneath it. (At the St Enoch Hotel, for example, a set of crockery was in use which sported the LMS arms with, beneath, the initials 'GSW'). As soon as the LMS Hotels Services assumed control in 1925 this arrangement was dropped and a laurel wreath device was adopted as standard. The elliptical version was probably the earlier and is certainly rarer than the circular. This style was used on silver, crockery, and glass. It was usually frosted into the glass but occasionally cut and filled with some kind of gold leaf or dye.

At a later date these devices were, in turn, displaced by a flowing and intertwining scroll rendering of the letters 'LMS'. The design is almost the same as that adopted for railwaymen's badges, carpets in first class carriages, and other railway equipment. (The discerning will have noticed the difference which is that, unlike the railway device, the 'L' of the hotels device is carried on beneath the 'M' instead of linking up with it). Sometimes the 'LMS' appeared on its own and sometimes with the words 'HOTELS', 'CARS', 'DINING CARS', or the name of a particular hotel, beneath it.

The latest style was a great deal simpler, consisting of plain sans serif letters within a rectangular frame. Almost every combination of the words 'HOTELS' and 'CARS' was used in conjunction with 'LMS'. Coincidentally the Director of Hotels adopted a design with the same plain rectangle, but set within a reeded ground which was known as the Lincoln Pattern. This was taken over by British Rail and many of the old LMS versions can be seen in use alongside the 'HE' and 'BTHS' ones. The same badging was also frosted onto the glassware. It was not widely used on LMS crockery, however, which was usually marked 'LMS HOTELS' or 'LM&S HOTELS' on the underside.

The Tea Room at St Pancras Hotel, London, photographed in about 1913.

LNW and LMS spoons, bearing the earlier scroll design with a later, more utilitarian fork. Rex Blaker Collection.

Above:
This handsome lettering was used for the LMS hotel china where every item down to the soap dish bore the device in crimson and gold on a white ground.
Left:
This effective design was used as a blocking on LMS stationery but also appeared on some crockery.

An interesting and ingenious variant was the very simple design used mainly on stationery and such things as leather blotting pads. The letters LMS were drawn, as far as possible, in straight lines to form the shape of a coffee pot which surmounted the word 'hotels'. Some examples of white, gold-lined, china have survived on which it appears in gold. Any example of its use on silverware would be extremely rare.

Turning now to the constituent companies, the LNWR was, of course, the largest. It was also the second largest hotel owner, operating seven hotels in England and Wales and controlling, through the DN&GR, one in Northern Ireland. Sadly, all but one of the company's hotels have now been closed or demolished to make way for the new electrified stations. Only the Crewe Arms Hotel at Crewe, now part of the Ind Coope Group, survives and this is fortunate as it is one of the earliest of the railway hotels. Under railway ownership it was a fascinating place. Because it made so little profit, the Crewe Arms was never modernised by the LMS and at the end of the war was the only railway hotel without running water in the bedrooms. Instead each room was equipped with a marble-topped wash-stand on which there reposed a large basin, cold water jug, soap-dish, and toothbrush dish, all in gold-lined white china and badged 'LMS' in red. In the morning the chambermaid would bring, in addition to the morning tea, a brass jug of hot water covered by a hand towel. By the time it was acquired by Walkers, the Warrington brewers, the hotel had become a railway relic in itself and they lost no time in modernising it and, incidentally, in

breaking up the equipment described above. Some of the brass jugs (marked 'LMS HOTELS' on the base) were retained and are still used as vases.

Nearly all LNWR silverware was badged with the Britannia emblem and, beneath, the name of the refreshment room or hotel to which it belonged. Sometimes, and especially on items belonging to the Marine Department, Britannia was surrounded by a garter bearing the initials 'L&NW Ry Co'. Marine Department ownership was indicated by the letters 'MD' in the tail of the garter. Whilst on the subject of this department it is worth mentioning the existence of a range of white crockery with a blue surround badged with a flag. Prince of Wales' feathers are superimposed on a cross on the flag and beneath it are the initials 'L&NW SS Co Ld'.

The North London Railway may be conveniently mentioned at this point as, from 1909 onwards, it was worked by the LNWR. The existence of cutlery badged with the LNWR emblem and the words 'BROAD ST REFT ROOMS' tends to indicate that it had no silverware of its own or that any which may have existed must now be extremely scarce.

The Midland Railway rightly prided itself on the standard of its catering facilities and it spared no expense when it came to equipping them. At least ten styles of badging were in use at various times and a sizeable collection could be made of Midland cutlery alone. The most impressive badging was that which featured the distinctive wyvern. Beneath it was the word 'MIDLAND' and, below that, a curved scroll containing the words 'RESTAURANT CARS'. The hotel edition of this consisted of the words 'MIDLAND

Even beer bottles bore the railway's stamp of owner-ship. Here an LMS bottle stands beside an earlier MR Co decanter. Cattell Collection.

RAILWAY HOTELS' in the scroll beneath the wyvern. Sometimes the curved scroll was used without the wyvern in which case the word 'HOTELS' was taken out of the scroll and placed beneath it. In a much rarer edition the wyvern is placed above an ornate monogram consisting of the letters 'MR' facing forwards, on the left, and backwards, on the right. Another range of Midland badging involves the use of garters on which are printed the words 'MIDLAND

RAILWAY HOTELS' or 'MIDLAND CARS'. Some-times 'MIDLAND RAILWAY' appears on the garter which surrounds the word 'HOTELS'. The Midland Hotel, Derby, was privileged to use a special badging in which 'MIDLAND HOTEL DERBY' appeared, as usual, on a garter but the whole was surmounted by a crown–presumably to commemorate the fact that Queen Victoria once stayed there. Some Midland cutlery is not badged at all on the front but merely has the name of one of the hotels stamped, in plain capitals, on the back. Most of this cutlery is of a very plain design but there is a more ornate version which has 'Mid Rly Hotels' stamped on the back in a cursive script.

Another large constituent company of the LMS was the Lancashire and Yorkshire. Most L&Y silver displayed the full coat of arms—often almost rididiculously large—and, although the company owned few hotels, a fair quantity of its silverware is still in use. Unfortunately, the arms were not very heavily stamped onto the silver and it is unusual to find an item which is not badly worn.

Moving now to Scotland we find that the three Scottish constituents were fairly lavish when it came to badging their equipment. The Caledonian and Glasgow & South Western displayed their full armorial devices on silverware, crockery, and even chamber pots. Unfortunately the Caledonian badging was subject to the same defect as that of the L&Y and clearly defined examples are not often seen. Although the Highland Railway used the full coat of arms on its chamber pots it apparently felt that it was not suitable for extensive use on its silverware. This is a great pity as the arms are attractive and would certainly have looked more impressive than the simple garters bearing the words 'THE HIGHLAND RAILWAY Co'.

Not many examples still exist to represent the other constituent companies of the LMS and it is doubtful if the smaller companies ever had any. Even the North Staffordshire Railway is unrepresented in most collections. One exception is the Furness Railway which adopted a badging of pleasing appearance consisting of the words 'FURNESS RAILWAY' surrounded by a garter bearing the words 'REFRESH-MENT DEPARTMENT'.

A third class dining car of the Midland Railway photographed in 1904.

The London and North Eastern Railway and its constituents

The two largest hotel owners in the LNER group were the Great Northern and North Eastern Railways both of which badged their hotel ware in a similar way. The badgings consisted of a garter bearing the words 'Gt NORTHERN RLY REFT ROOMS' (or simply 'GNH') or 'NER REFRESHMENT ROOMS' with the name of the hotel or station of origin inside the garter. On the NER the garter was occasionally oval. This style was adopted by the LNER as standard in the early days but, later, it gave way to a less ornate form. In addition to the above the LNER employed a seemingly endless variety of plain markings. The most casual collector will not have to look far before he comes across examples with 'LONDON & NORTH EASTERN RAILWAY' in full along the handle or with the initials 'LNER RC GE' indicating that the cutlery was intended for use only on restaurant cars running on the Great Eastern Section. It is not surprising that this expensive practice of badging equipment for use in a particular place was eventually abandoned in favour of stamping it simply 'LNER' in script so that it could be ordered in bulk and used anywhere on the system. A very large amount of silver badged in this way is still in use.

Monograms appear to have been used exclusively on china and glass, though the Great Northern used a 'GNR' on its silverware. The North Eastern which, like the Highland Railway, preferred garters to coats of arms where silver was concerned had no hesitation in using the full arms, in a multi-coloured version, on its crockery. Beneath the arms the words 'NE Ry HOTELS DEPT' appeared in a scroll. Not to be outdone, the Great Northern caused its device to appear on crockery with 'GREAT NORTHERN RAILWAY' above and 'REFRESHMENT DEPARTMENT' below but, unlike the North Eastern, it apparently felt unable to run to more than one colour.

In July 1937 the streamlined 'Coronation' train went into service between Kings Cross and Edinburgh. The specially designed set of coaches was provided with electrically operated air conditioning and every effort was made to achieve silent travel. To this end a new set of cutlery was produced with flat handles to prevent rattling on the tables. All of this cutlery, and the special plain blue-grey crockery which accompanied it, was badged with the 'high-speed' design. The crockery and glassware, made by Minton and the Edinburgh Crystal Glass Company respectively, must have cost a small fortune.

The LNER inherited four hotels from the Great Eastern Railway but only one, at Liverpool Street Station, is still open today. Not famed for its rail services the GER, was, however, noted for its catering

This decorative LNER monogram appeared on china and glass throughout the system.
An NER garter design for the plate at York Station Hotel. Rex Blaker Collection.

facilities. Great Eastern relics are not scarce, especially in East Anglia, and may easily be recognised by the dragon's wing (adopted by the GER from the City of London crest). One of the last genuine station dining rooms to be closed was that at Norwich and this yielded up a hoard of collectors' pieces, all bearing the GER badging, and mostly in good condition. Glassware was simply marked with the initials 'GER' which were frosted into it.

One of the smallest constituent companies was the Great North of Scotland Railway which, nevertheless, was the proud owner of two hotels, the Cruden Bay and the Palace Hotels, Aberdeen, both now demolished. The GNS probably never owned a great deal of silver but one collectors' piece which has survived is a plain but attractive bread boat bearing the full coat of arms of the company (itself a scarce item). The arms are surrounded by a garter on which are the words 'GREAT NORTH OF SCOTLAND RAILWAY Co ABERDEEN' and beneath all this is stamped 'REFRESHMENT ROOMS ABERDEEN'. Cutlery was more simply badged within an oval.

Items from the other Scottish constituent, the North British Railway, are in equally short supply. One magnificent survivor is a small teapot badged with the full coat of arms surrounded by a garter bearing the words 'THE NORTH BRITISH STATION HOTEL EDINBURGH'. Below this are the letters 'RC'.

Leaving aside the smaller constituents, there remain only the Great Central Railway and its forbear the Manchester, Sheffield, & Lincolnshire. Both companies bequeathed a considerable quantity of silverware to the LNER much of which is still in circulation. The MS&L operated a number of hotels but the GCR was so impoverished by the time of the London extension that it was unable to open the hotels planned for Nottingham and London. The MS&L silverware was not very inspiring. It was badged with the name of a station surrounded by a garter with the company's initials. By way of contrast the GCR put into service the most magnificently badged range of any railway company. On literally every item there appeared the full coat of arms, resplendent with its locomotive crest, with 'Gt CENTRAL Ry' above and a station name or

'DINING CAR' below it. The china and glassware was similarly embellished. Unfortunately, like that of the L&Y and Caledonian Railways, the badging rubbed smooth very quickly and clear-cut examples are rare. There were at least two alternative GCR designs, both of which involved the use of garters. In one the initials 'GCR' appeared on an oval or circular garter which surrounded the single initial 'I' or 'M' or 'W' etc. In another alternative the full name of the Company, on a garter, surrounded the initials of an hotel, 'Y.G.', for example, standing for the Yarborough Hotel, Grimsby.

The Great Western Railway and its constituents
In its later years the GWR operated only five hotels and, as the third largest of the four great companies, had fewer dining and refreshment rooms than the LMS and LNER. It is therefore pleasantly surprising to find that so much GWR equipment has survived. Much of the silverware carries the well-known London and Bristol arms with 'GREAT WESTERN RAILWAY HOTELS' in a scroll beneath. In the case of restaurant car equipment the initials 'GWR' appeared beneath the arms and, beneath these, a scroll bearing the words, 'RESTAURANT CARS'. Only two other basic designs were used. The earlier consists of the GWR monogram within a garter bearing the words 'REFRESHMENT DEPARTMENT', 'DINING CAR', or the name of an hotel. The latest design, which was first used in the mid-1930s features the initials GWR within a plain circle. This is the most common, but crested silverware comes a close second. The Great Western appears to have had a liking for pewter tankards and measures, many of which are still in use. Another curious survival is a range of cutlery issued for use with luncheon baskets. These are badged 'R D' surrounded by an oval carrying the words 'GWR LUNCHEON BASKET'. Relics originating with the Great Western's constituent companies are very rare.

The Southern Railway and its constituents
The Southern, like the GWR, operated very few hotels and today only the Charing Cross Hotel in London remains. Three different types of SR badging may still be found. Firstly there is the almost inevitable garter bearing the name 'SOUTHERN RAILWAY'. The second type is much more interesting consisting of the letters 'SR' with an electric flash running between them. This is, of course, nothing more than the standard SR emblem for the 'Southern Electric' but, above it, there is depicted on the cutlery an electric motor coach about $\frac{7}{8}$in length. The final design is made up simply of the letters 'SR' in what has been described as 'sunshine lettering'.

The LSWR is, perhaps the best represented of the Southern constituents and the LBSCR the worst.

An early LNER soup spoon and the Coronation fork of 1937 with its 'highspeed' design. Rex Blaker Collection.

Examples of the LSW badging—an elaborate cursive monogram—may be found still in service as may examples of an alternative consisting of the company's initials in a kind of Gothic lettering. A similar badging consisting only of the letters 'SWR' may also come to light.

This GWR monogram within a garter contrasts with the simple design of the mid 1930s. Rex Blaker Collection.

Southern Railway plate. Left: the ubiquitous garter, centre: the Southern Electric design complete with electric motor coach and right: SR's 'sunshine' lettering. Rex Blaker Collection.

The LC&DR badged all its silver with the full heraldic device to which was added, for good measure, the company's initials. This despite the fact that the name 'LONDON CHATHAM & DOVER RAILWAY COMPANY' was written in full round the device.

Special hotel ware was provided by the Southern and its constituents for their steamships. In the case of the LBSCR the house flag was featured in the centre of a garter bearing the company's initials and the name of the ship. The Southern omitted both garter and ship's name and had merely the flag surmounting a scroll in which the name of the company appeared.

The 'Lincoln pattern' devised for LMS was adopted first by the Hotels Executive of British Rail and subsequently by BTHS. Rex Blaker Collection.

The Hotels Executive and British Transport Hotels
Upon nationalisation the railways became the responsibility of the Railway Executive and their former catering interests were hived off to become the responsibility of a separate body – the Hotels Executive. Several hotels were sold or closed within the first few years and the dining rooms followed shortly afterwards. As a result only twenty-nine of the hotels are now left and the genuine station dining room has ceased to exist.

The LMS Lincoln Pattern cutlery was adopted as standard and this soon made its appearance badged 'HOTELS HE' or 'CARS HE'. Similarly the LMS coloured crockery, the 'Royal Scot' Pattern, was chosen as standard and sets of this were produced as soon after the war as the manufacture of patterned crockery was permitted. This did not last long. Under nationalisation the passenger has had to make do with cardboard beakers and plates and a variety of commonplace plastic implements.

Under the Beeching re-organisation the Hotels Executive was abolished and its undertaking transferred to a newly-formed limited company, British Transport Hotels Limited. Since this body took over, the rapid deterioration in the standards of refreshment room and train catering has been halted. Even the 'disposable' plastic teaspoons are gradually being replaced by metal ones bearing the BR 'arrows' symbol.

In the railway hotels the standards of the old companies are being maintained and, in some cases, even overtaken. It is to be hoped, however, that the stainless steel cutlery now in use on the trains will not gain admittance to the hotels. Not much HE cutlery is now in evidence and the BTHS badging is seen more and more frequently. It is probably true to say, though, that there is as much pre-nationalisation silverware in present use as there is BTHS.

Special and Jointly-owned Ware
Reference has already been made to the fact that the GNR and NER issued each of their hotels with specially-badged silverware but this was also true of a number of other establishments. The most obvious example is Gleneagles which, when it was opened in 1924, was equipped with its own cutlery, china, and glass. Other hotels with special badgings were the Euston whose rather plain cutlery had 'EUSTON HOTEL' stamped on the back. At the other extreme its neighbour, the Midland Grand at St Pancras, boasted silverware designed, as far as possible, to match the architecture of the building with the hotel name in Gothic lettering. As if this were not enough the Midland wyvern badge and scroll were added to certain items. The hotel cutlery had a special badge consisting of a scroll, bearing the name of the hotel in full, which zig-zagged its way down the handle. A similar zig-zag pattern was designed for Carlisle Citadel Station. Mention must also be made of the Furness Abbey, with its gothic lettering; the Charing Cross, which incorporated a Maltese Cross; the Station Hotel, Perth, which sported a garter bearing the 'STATION HOTEL' wording with 'PERTH' in the centre; the Royal Victoria, Sheffield, with three sheaves to represent Sheffield surmounted by the hotel's name in capital letters; and the Park Hotel, Preston. The latter adopted the insignia of the North Union Railway which, in turn, had been adopted from the arms of Preston itself. Special badgings were also used on dining car ware and the most common examples are to be found on cutlery belonging to the owners of the West and East Coast Joint Stock.

Acquisition of Cutlery, China and Glass
Railway cutlery, china and glass are not easy to obtain. Good quality plate will last almost indefinitely and, if the plate wears thin or the article becomes too badly dented for further use, it can be beaten out, replated, re-badged, and put back into service. For this reason British Transport Hotels and their predecessors have steadfastly refused to sell—except in the case of very damaged pieces. From time to time small quantities of badged ware which were surplus to requirements have been sold to collectors. Some of these items have found their way into dealers' shops where they can be bought—at a price commensurate with their rarity. Two encouraging innovations have been made in recent years. Firstly some very interesting items (which were not under the control of BTHS) have been released from time to time to Collectors' Corner at Euston. Secondly British Transport Hotels have themselves realised that there is a growing interest in their property and surplus items are now on sale (at fairly high prices) in some of their hotels.

This group includes a cup and saucer for one of SR's steamships and bears the house flag. Cattell Collection.

Carriage Panels

George Dow

It is only in recent years that the carriage panel has attracted the attention of the collector of railwayana. In consequence, a great deal of interesting early art-work in this sphere has disappeared and has not even survived in museums.

The most popular form of decoration was the photograph of a beauty spot or resort served by the railway. The Midland, Great Central, South Western, South Eastern & Chatham, North Staffordshire, North

Western and Great Western trains all indulged in this type of illustration together with some other companies.

After grouping, the practice was continued by the London Midland & Scottish and the Great Western, with sepia photographs by the former and black and white by the latter. The Great Western also introduced a system map printed in red, white and blue. It was geographic in design and, because the shape of the system was incompatible with landscape treatment, it was severely distorted. Both the London & North

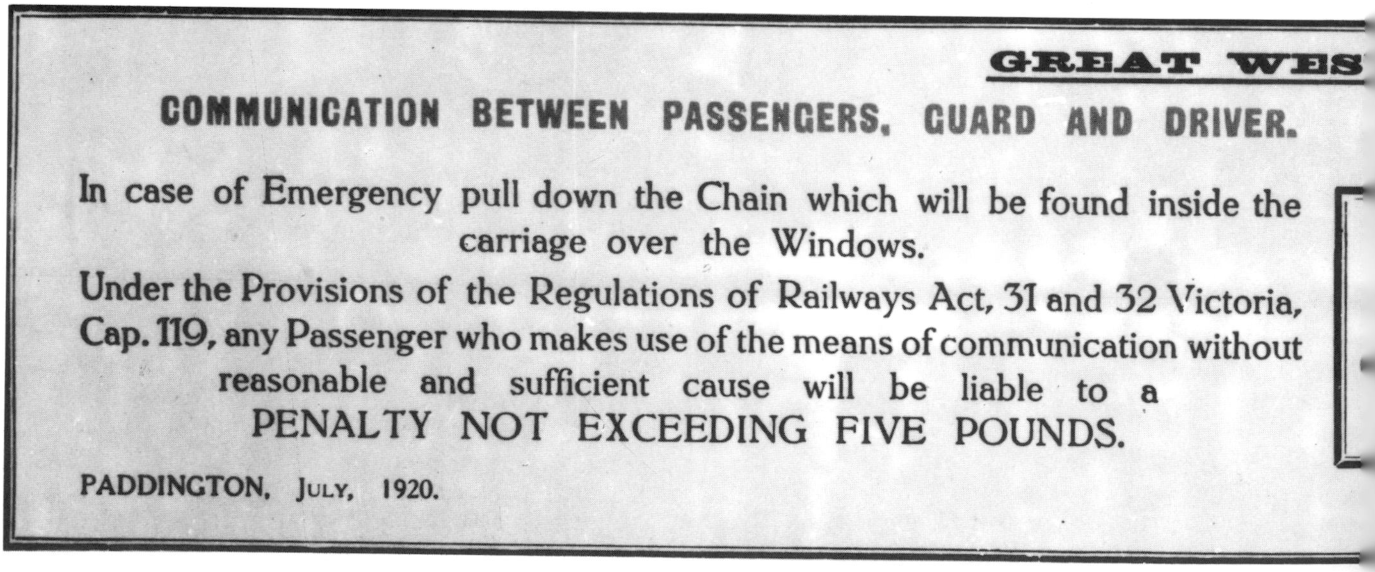

GWR carriage notice for July, 1920.

GREAT WES

COMMUNICATION BETWEEN PASSENGERS, GUARD AND DRIVER.

In case of Emergency pull down the Chain which will be found inside the carriage over the Windows.

Under the Provisions of the Regulations of Railways Act, 31 and 32 Victoria, Cap. 119, any Passenger who makes use of the means of communication without reasonable and sufficient cause will be liable to a **PENALTY NOT EXCEEDING FIVE POUNDS.**

PADDINGTON, JULY, 1920.

Eastern and Southern preferred the less expensive scenic views painted by eminent artists and printed in colour.

One of the first, if not the first, railway companies to display maps in its carriages was the Great Eastern, whose classic printed colour panel is reproduced. This dates back to the early 1900s and was a feature of all main line compartments. It will be seen that three maps were included in the design, covering the suburban network (on which eventually the world's most intensive steam hauled train services were to be operated), the main lines and branches, and the Broads area. Splashes of colour were provided by sketches of a blue 4–4–0 locomotive, a red and cream double decker bus (both of which had been built at Stratford works), a Continental steamship of the company, its armorial device and a sailing boat.

Carriage panels made up of transfers mounted on boards were also in vogue in the pre-grouping years, especially in Great Northern and North Eastern main line trains, and in the coaches of East Coast Joint Stock, which were owned by these two railways, along with the North British. They were chiefly used to advertise railway hotels, and the Great Northern example is typical. The North Eastern designs advertised its hotels at York, Newcastle and Hull and bore at the base the legend 'Dinner is ready at York on arrival of the Scotch expresses which are allowed not less than 20 minutes in the station', a reminder of the days before corridor trains and restaurant cars.

Diagrammatic maps in trains were given their greatest impetus by the models of clarity which appeared in London Underground trains during the distinguished *régime* of Frank Pick at 55 Broadway. Few administrators have been blessed with an equal determination to implement good design in all forms of railway equipment. During the grouping years diagrammatic maps, designed by the author, were produced by the LNER for the steam trains operating on the London suburban lines of the Great Central, Great Northern and Great Eastern sections and for the electric trains on the Tyneside and Manchester–Altrincham lines. On the LMS a diagrammatic map of the Tilbury and Southend lines, also of the author's design, was to be seen in trains into and out of Fenchurch Street. The Southern displayed in electric stock a map of its complex suburban area, but this was geographic and not diagrammatic in design.

In the early years of nationalisation a cheaper alternative had to be found by the London Midland for the sepia photographs, which were not only then costing 7/6d (37½p) each but were, in some cases, hopelessly out of date. The adoption of the much more economic carriage panel, printed in colour, was justified because the large fleet of LMS coaches, with their extra wide carriage panel spaces, then ran into thousands and had still some years of useful life ahead of them.

A series of orthodox scenic views printed in colour in the LNER manner was accordingly produced. The author commissioned C. Hamilton Ellis to paint in oils a couple of dozen pre-grouping scenes on the English components of the LMS. At the same time two other eminent artists, Claude Buckle and Kenneth Steel, were given the job of painting a like number of railway architectural features. The subjects selected gave an emphasis, deliberately, to features not wholly visible from the train, such as bridges, viaducts and ornamental tunnel portals.

Two examples of these railway scenes, the historic London & Birmingham mail train and the decorative Red Hill tunnel entrances at Trent Junction, are reproduced. Their appearance was so appreciated by

N RAILWAY.

COLD LUNCHEON and TEA BASKETS MAY BE —— OBTAINED AT:

PADDINGTON	BRISTOL	CARDIFF	BIRMINGHAM (Snow Hill)
*SLOUGH	CHEDDAR	NEATH	BANBURY
WINDSOR	WESTON-SUPER-MARE	LANDORE	LEAMINGTON
*MAIDENHEAD	TAUNTON	TENBY	STRATFORD-ON-AVON
READING	EXETER	CARMARTHEN	DUDLEY
NEWBURY	NEWTON ABBOT	*FISHGUARD HARBOUR	KIDDERMINSTER
WESTBURY (Wilts.)	TORQUAY	PONTYPOOL ROAD	WOLVERHAMPTON L.L.
*WEYMOUTH QUAY	PLYMOUTH (N. RD.)	GLOUCESTER	WELLINGTON (Salop)
DIDCOT	PLYMOUTH (M.B.)	HEREFORD (Barrs Court)	CRAVEN ARMS
SWINDON	PLYMOUTH DOCKS	GREAT MALVERN	SHREWSBURY
CHIPPENHAM	TRURO	LEDBURY	RUABON
TROWBRIDGE	PENZANCE	WORCESTER (Shrub Hill)	CHESTER
BATH	NEWPORT	OXFORD	

* TEA BASKETS ONLY SUPPLIED AT THESE STATIONS.

railway enthusiasts that folders of four subjects were made up for sale. Today these early examples of British railway art have become collectors' pieces.

For trains which were confined to set services the diagrammatic map returned as a carriage panel. These services were, of course, those provided by electric cars on the Lancaster–Heysham–Morecambe, Mersey & Wirral, Manchester–Altrincham, Manchester–Bury and Liverpool–Southport lines. The maps were executed in a standardised style, printed in maroon and black on white paper or card and embellished with the British Railways original lozenge-shaped totem. The

BR carriage route diagram. George Dow Collection.
C. Hamilton Ellis's Travel in 1905.

aim of their design was to make them the equal of the best the London Underground could offer, and in this it is believed that the draughtsman, Victor Welch, was successful. A typical example, covering electric lines out of Euston and Broad Street is reproduced.

One other carriage panel venture of the early years of nationalisation is worthy of mention. This was the mirror map, believed to be the only one of its kind used on railways in this country. Several thousand of them were made by Novolor Ltd to the author's requirements for display centrally below the luggage racks in LMS-type main line stock. These mirror maps, which have now all disappeared, depict a time when three trunk lines into London, the Midland, North Western and Great Central, were operated by the London Midland.

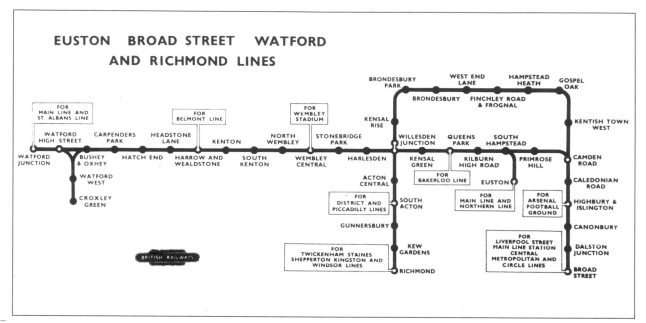

Opposite page:
GER carriage map.
GNR panel advertising the company's hotels.
Kenneth Steel's painting of the Red Hill tunnels.
C. Hamilton Ellis's Travel in 1845.
All George Dow Collection.

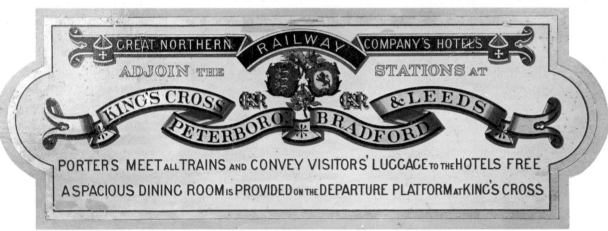

Top row, left to right: *Newcastle & Carlisle Railway handpainted armorial device. National Railway Museum. London Brighton & South Coast Railway handpainted armorial device. Museum of Science and Engineering, Newcastle. LNWR and L&Y Joint, to the left Britannia and on the right the arms of Lancaster and York. P. B. Whitehouse Collection. Second row: Caledonian Railway emblem with the Scottish coat of arms. P. B. Whitehouse Collection. Great Central coat of arms,* *granted in 1898. George Dow Collection. Southern Railway coat of arms. George Dow Collection. Third row: Ulster Transport Authority. George Dow Collection. Great Western Railway. P. B. Whitehouse Collection. London, Midland & Scottish Railway. P. B. Whitehouse Collection. Fourth row: Midland Railway, Central London Railway and Festiniog Railway All P. B. Whitehouse Collection.*

Heraldry

George Dow

The feudal character of the railways of this country during their formative years is reflected in their use of heraldic devices to denote ownership and as a means of decoration. Initially heraldry was frequently embodied, in one form or another, in the company's seal, which was brought into use for the completion of legal documents immediately the Act of Incorporation received the Royal Assent. From the seal stemmed the company's armorial device (too often wrongly described by railway enthusiasts as a crest), which sometimes appeared as a decorative feature in the stonework of structures, such as stations, or in the ironwork of bridges or station roof supports, as the construction of the railway proceeded. A few are still to be seen.

By the time the railway was completed the armorial device was most prolific in headed stationery and on staff uniforms, either as cap badges or on buttons, which were made of horn, copper, German nickel, silver or brass. Hand painted in full heraldic colours, it also adorned the doors or bodies of 1st class coaches. The survival of such buttons or badges from those early days is almost entirely due to the efforts of private collectors. Rare specimens include a silver finished button of the London & Brighton Railway, embodying shields representing the places in the title set beneath the Royal crown, and a nickel silver button of the City & South London, the first tube railway in the world. A dragon or wyvern surmounts the London arms and Southwark cross.

Several excellent specimens of hand painted armorial devices have, fortunately, been preserved in museums.

The two reproduced are probably the only examples of their kind still in existence. The beautiful device of the Newcastle & Carlisle Railway shows two superb seahorses supporting the arms of Newcastle (*left*) and Carlisle (*right*) beneath the crest of the first-named. The other is the ornate first device of the London, Brighton & South Coast, successor to the London & Brighton. This is one of the earliest to incorporate a locomotive as a crest. The shield contains parts of the arms of London (*top*), the Cinque Ports (*right*), Portsmouth (*left*) and Brighton (*bottom*). The supporters are dragons from the arms of London. Beneath the title is an appendage bearing the initials JCC, indicating that the vehicle wearing the device was an inspection coach of J. C. Craven, the Locomotive & Carriage Superintendent.

In 1856 the Birmingham firm of Tearne & Sons Ltd invented the transfer, which at once offered an economical and much more speedily applied alternative to hand painting devices in colour. The armorial embellishment not only of coaches but also of locomotives could now be undertaken on a grand scale, and this is exactly what happened. Many coaches henceforth displayed two devices on each side, below the waist, sometimes supplemented on the waist by ornate gilt monograms of the railway's initials. On locomotives the device might be transferred to the leading or centre coupled wheel splashers, or to tender and tank sides. Some railways, especially in Ireland and Wales, favoured a position high up on the cab sides.

Bearing in mind that no authority was sought or

Silver button made for the London & Brighton Railway in 1837. David Swan Collection.

Silver plated nickel button made for the City and South London Railway. David Swan Collection.

Silver plated whistle made for the West Lancashire Railway. National Railway Museum.

LNER hand painted coat of arms.
National Railway Museum.

given for these armorial bearings the blatancy of some of the designs was unbelievable. The Liverpool & Manchester share certificates had carried a representation of Britannia and the London & Birmingham included a statue of her in the noble Great Hall of old Euston. After these and other lines were merged to form the London & North Western Railway in 1846, Britannia, as much a British symbol as her guardian lion or John Bull, became the universal emblem of the company. Its northern ally, the Caledonian, went one better; it calmly annexed the Scottish coat of arms as its heraldic device! But one railway did not have things all its own way. The Great Northern, which embodied the full achievement of the City of London in its first design, eventually got into such hot water with the College of Arms that an entirely new emblem had to be introduced.

Although the directors of the nascent Manchester, Sheffield & Lincolnshire were known to have consulted the College of Arms over the design of its seal (and a few other companies may have done likewise) no grant of arms was made to any railway company until 25th February 1898. On this historic date the Manchester, Sheffield & Lincolnshire, having changed its name to Great Central a few months earlier, was granted a coat of arms by the Garter, Clarenceux and Norroy Kings at Arms. It is a pleasant, almost austere design. Appropriately, a winged locomotive forms the crest, a harbinger of the high speeds attained by the Great Central 20th-century expresses. The upper part of the shield embodies, left to right, parts of the arms of Manchester, Sheffield and Lincoln; beneath are a pair of wyvern's wings from the crest of Leicester, with a hollow cross and short swords to represent London, together with the winged cap of Mercury to underline speedy transport; and at the base a scroll bearing the word *Forward* provided an apt motto for a progressive company. The motto is also that of Birmingham, which Great Central metals were destined never to reach.

Since 1898 only four transport undertakings have been granted armorial bearings. They were, successively, the London & North Eastern Railway, the Southern Railway, the British Transport Commission and the Ulster Transport Authority. All four are illustrated and it will be noticed that in two cases the motto *Forward* was adopted.

Unfortunately no transfers were made of the LNER and Southern achievements. The former was one of the most beautiful ever displayed by a railway company. It was painted in full colours on but two locomotives and never adorned passenger rolling stock. Its most frequent appearance was on stationery and uniform buttons. Mercury, issuing from clouds of steam, forms the crest. St George's cross of London, bearing the four

lions of York and the castle of Edinburgh, divided the shield. The Anglo-Scottish character of the system is emphasised by the inclusion of two London griffins, a rose and a thistle in the four quarters. And two magnificent lions, one wearing a collar of roses and the other a collar of thistles, act as the supporters.

More than two decades elapsed before the achievement of the Southern made its début. Its display was even more restricted, for it appeared only on one or two official publications and, in the form of coloured vitreous enamel plates, on each side of the Pacific locomotive No 34090 *Sir Eustace Missenden*. An unusual feature is the multiple crest, which embodies a double disc steam locomotive wheel pierced by a flash to denote electric traction and winged to indicate speedy transport; behind is the sun, to remind one of the slogan *South for Sunshine*. The red dragon of London and white horse of Kent are supporters and the shield, which has a field of heraldic water to represent the coastal areas served, carries smaller shields with emblems representing London (sword), Dover (leopard's head), Brighton (dolphin) and Southampton (rose).

The achievement of the British Transport Commission is an equally striking design. Here the crest is in the form of a demi-lion rampant holding a wheel between its paws. The shield, which is largely coloured green to denote the countryside, contains three wheels at the top to denote the railways and a chained portcullis at the base to indicate the ports and harbours, whilst across the centre are straight and wavy bands to represent railways, roads and waterways. The second motto, *Velociter securiter—Swift and sure*, is an apt touch.

An adaptation of the crest was made in transfer form for locomotives and coaches, and there was a particularly handsome version in chrome finished metal for the London Midland electric locomotives. In the coach transfer the crown from which the demi-lion is *issuant* embodies the English rose, the Scottish thistle, the Welsh leek and the oak to represent all Great Britain.

In 1960 the Ulster Transport Authority was granted its fine achievement. A flying horse, charged with the dexter red hand of Ulster, forms the crest. The green shield, which symbolises Northern Ireland, carries a diagonal band to denote railways and roads, flanked by the six counties in the form of coronets. The supporting lion and elk, which wear mural crowns around their necks to represent the boroughs of Belfast and Derry, connote the associations of the province with the United Kingdom and Ireland.

Two of the best known of the unauthorised devices are those of the Great Western and London Midland & Scottish Railways. The basic design of the first-named dates back to the incorporation of the company

Original artwork for the British Transport coat of arms as granted by the College of Arms.

Lynton & Barnstaple armorial transfer. National Railway Museum.

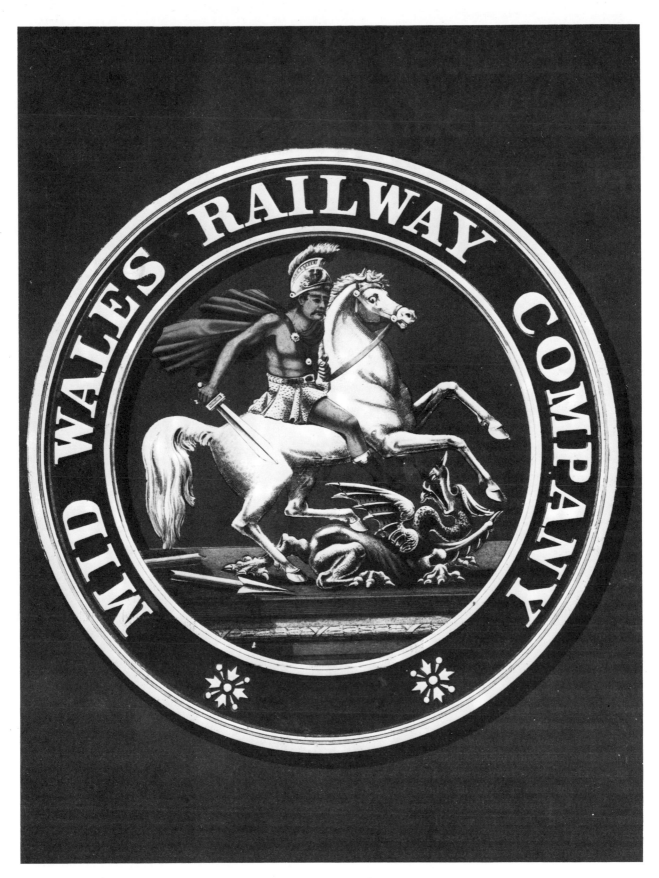

Mid Wales armorial transfer. George Dow Collection.

in 1835, when Parliamentary sanction was given for the construction of a railway between London and Bristol. Parts of the achievements of these two cities were adapted as an insignia. And there they remained until nationalisation in 1948, despite the great growth of the system up to the 20th century and its grouping with several vigorous and enterprising Welsh railways in 1923. There was some minor variation in the design over the years. The fourth and final transfer of 1928 was applied to locomotives and coaches alike.

The armorial transfer of the LMS also failed, like that of the Great Western, to portray the extent of the system represented. It was the biggest of all four grouped railways and was content to display, within a circle 14⅛ inches in diameter, merely the dragon's wing of London and a rose and thistle motif to denote England and Scotland. Yet the company's two leading constituents, the Midland and the London & North Western, owned lines in the four countries of the United Kingdom!

Whilst the LNWR flaunted Britannia as its insignia and called itself *The Premier Line*, the Midland, more subtle with the slogan *The Best Way*, displayed a geographical transfer which, in its final form, was one of the most attractive of the pre-grouping armorial devices. The wyvern, inherited from an ancestor, the Leicester & Swannington, made a distinctive crest. The shield, which was supported by a dolphin and a salamander, was divided into six parts which denoted, left to right, Birmingham, Derby and Bristol in the upper half and Leicester, Lincoln and Leeds in the bottom. It adorned passenger and goods tender locomotives, even when the latter assumed unlined black as a livery in place of crimson lake.

Much earlier a device embodying a shield divided into five parts had appeared on two issues of uniform buttons. The five places represented were Leicester, Derby and Nottingham in the top half, with Birmingham and Leeds beneath.

The wyvern became the universal symbol of the Midland and was as instantly recognisable as the evergreen bar and circle symbol of London Transport was to become in later years. It was most in use as a cap badge and as the central motif of uniform buttons, but it was also to be seen on timetable covers and other publications, in compartment luggage rack supports, in stone and metal structures and on hotel china.

There are some further designs which are worthy of comment in this brief survey of a decorative practice which the British have made their own. First, the device of the Lynton & Barnstaple, of which only one specimen is known to exist. This delightful narrow gauge line, closed in 1935, displayed upon the sides of its diminutive coaches a charmingly simple insignia. Within the garter are shields bearing a castle and a stag denoting Barnstaple and Exmoor respectively. They were taken from the company's seal.

The Central London Railway provides the only known case of a British railway armorial device embodying representations of two parishes; furthermore, it shared only with the Maryport & Carlisle Railway the distinction of bearing neither name nor motto. The crest is, of course, taken from the City of London achievement, as is the first quarter, and in the fourth quarter is denoted the county of Middlesex. The two parishes represented are those of St George, Hanover Square (St George and the dragon) and St Marylebone (The Virgin and Child).

St George and the dragon constituted the sole motif of the emblem of the little Mid Wales Railway. It is totally different from the version in the Central London arms, and is, in fact, virtually a copy of Benedetto Pistrucci's renowned design for the British coinage of yesteryear, notably the gold sovereign. Its significance has not yet been discovered. The Mid Wales, often somewhat impoverished, certainly served no Klondyke!

The Mid Wales was absorbed in 1888 (hence the great rarity of its device) by the Cambrian Railways, the longest Welsh system. The Cambrian produced a pair of excellent and unusual examples of its first ventures into heraldry in the brickwork of two of the gable ends of its station at Frankton; these are still extant, although the station was closed in 1964. It will be observed that the company's title was wrongly rendered in the singular. The shield within the trefoil is shared by a Welsh dragon and an English rose, the latter because of the Cambrian's incursion into Shropshire.

Today British Railways eschew heraldry. The emphasis is on symbolism, coupled with emasculation of designation, such as British Rail and Merseyrail, and the symbolism set the current tawdry fashion which can appropriately be described as 'arrowmania'. It has been left to the independent small or preserved railways to carry on the armorial tradition, amongst which are the Talyllyn, the Festiniog, the Keighley & Worth Valley, the Dart Valley and the Romney, Hythe & Dymchurch. Two are worth noting, representing the emblemmatic and heraldic respectively.

The Fairbourne, another narrow gauge line, which was opened in West Wales as long ago as 1890 shows within a roundel of 6in diameter the red Welsh dragon as the central feature. The background is made up of heraldic water, greensward and mountain, the latter superimposed on the spokes of a wheel. This transfer ornaments most of the locomotives and coaches. The preserved standard gauge steam-operated Bluebell Railway, once part of the Sheffield Park–Horsted Keynes section of the Southern has evolved an attrac-

Coat of arms of the Cambrian Railways on a gable end at Frankton Station.

tive armorial device, worn by locomotive No 323 *Bluebell*. The shield is quartered by the crest of the Holroyd family, whose seat of Sheffield Park was served by the station of that name, now the headquarters of the line; the arms of Lewes; the arms of East Grinstead Urban District; and, in the fourth quarter, the arms of the Norman family of Cahaignes, from which Horsted Keynes is derived. There is no crest, but the motto, *Floreat Vapor*, (*May Steam Flourish*) which could hardly be more appropriate.

To start any collection nowadays of railway heraldic endeavour is no mean task, particularly if one rejects current commercial imitations on the market, some of which are inaccurate. Uniform buttons, armorially embellished, probably afford the field least tilled of all, and a sizeable collection occupies little space. Then

there are timetables, the covers of which often carried the arms of the issuing railway company, sometimes in colour, and highly interesting also because of their content of bygone train services of great variety. If one has the wall space available the genuine armorial transfer, mounted on a plaque finished in the appropriate locomotive or coach colour, is undoubtedly the most decorative of all. A group of half a dozen makes an arresting splash of colour. Most specimens are now difficult and a little expensive to acquire, but at least they offer a good investment.

Apart from collections in private hands and that owned by the Railway Club, the most comprehensive armorial display available for public inspection is in the National Railway Museum now at York. There are two much smaller displays in London, both worth a visit, in the Science Museum, South Kensington and in the Railway Tavern, Liverpool Street.

Nameplates, Number Plates, Shed Plates and Works Plates

H. C. Casserley

The first steam locomotive to run on rails, Trevithick's Pen-y-darran engine, was merely an experimental piece of machinery; not unnaturally it hardly warranted the bestowal of any form of special name.

A few years later, engines for colliery work were produced by William Hedley and George Stephenson. Two, which appeared in 1812 and 1813 (still in existence in museums) were known as *Wylam Dilly* and *Puffing Billy*, but these were probably local nicknames; there is no evidence that the names were ever displayed in any way. The first engine deliberately to carry a name seems to have been Stephenson's celebrated *Locomotion No 1* of 1825 for the Stockton & Darlington Railway; it was also the first to bear a number, both being carried on the side of the boiler. As the number of locomotives began to increase, some method of distinguishing them verbally and in documentation obviously became necessary. At first this was often by names alone, but the Stockton & Darlington continued to add numbers and by 1827 had reached No 5 *Royal George*, built by Timothy Hackworth. The Liverpool & Manchester Railway, commencing with the famous *Rocket* of 1829, had a total of 69 engines by 1839, all bearing names; the later machines were numbered, but it is not clear whether the first few actually carried them. It seems unlikely that the *Rocket* was numbered as no early illustrations of the time show this. Stephenson must have liked the name, as he had already produced a *Rocket No 7* for the Stockton & Darlington in 1827.

Thus the practice of naming and numbering engines grew through the years, usually in the form of a single brass plate attached to the boiler barrel, but later names were more often to be found as curved plates on the driving wheel splashers whilst the number tended to be transferred to the cabside. Some railways eventually economised on the production of plates by painting the names and numbers on the engines, which practice, although not strictly coming within the context of this review, must inevitably warrant passing reference.

With the creation of the major companies around the middle of the 19th century, the practice of naming varied considerably amongst the lines concerned. So far as overseas railways were concerned, the habit of bestowing names never really caught on to the extent that it did at home. Even in Great Britain and Ireland, the practice differed enormously; some railways, such as the Midland and the Great Northern, throughout their independent existences only gave names to two of their locomotives, the latter bestowing the second just before its absorption into the LNER. The North Eastern was in a similar position, while the Great Eastern could boast but three, and the Glasgow & South Western one. Other railways, such as the Lancashire & Yorkshire and the London & South Western, abandoned naming at a very early stage, except for a few miscellaneous tank engines in the case of the latter company. At the other extreme, two of the largest railways in England and in Ireland adopted naming on a large scale. In Ireland the Midland Great Western and the Great Northern of Ireland (although

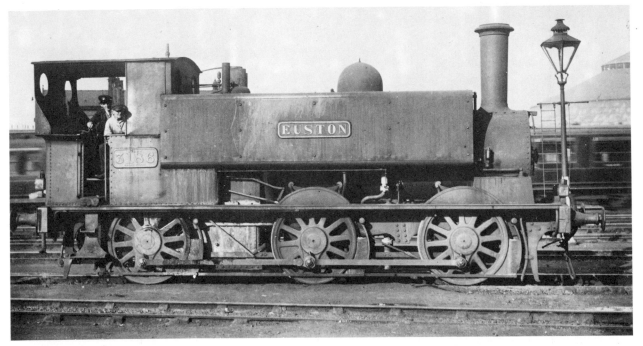

LNWR Shark. *Prince of Wales class.*
LNWR Euston. *Special dock tank.*
GWR Bride of Lammermoor. *Saint class.*

largely discontinued in later years) were prolific namers. At home the London & North Western and the Great Western, followed this practice to the end of their independent existences (in the case of the GWR this lasted until nationalisation in 1948, and even persisted for a few more years under British Railways).

To take the LNWR first, the standard form of nameplate had its origin in Trevithick's *Cornwall* of 1847, and was perpetuated with little alteration through the superintendencies of Alexander Allan, John Ramsbottom, F. W. Webb, George Whale, C. J. Bowen Cooke, and Montague Beames until 1921. It consisted of a curved brass plate mounted on the splashers, with the name in stamped recessed lettering, painted black, together with, from Webb days, the legend at either extremity, 'Crewe Works' with the date of construction or rebuild. Later designs of engines necessitated the use of a straight plate. As the practice of naming was confined to express tender types, the question of application to tank engines did not arise, with two interesting exceptions, a couple of pannier tanks, *Euston* and *Liverpool*, which had larger plates more in line with the standard number plates. These engines were used to take boat trains through the stygian tunnels from Edgehill to Liverpool Riverside station.

The standard GWR nameplate was a rather more imposing affair than that of the LNWR, with handsome raised letters in serif characters which remained the same right to the end, never changing to the plainer type or to the extremely austere Gill Sans style which became more fashionable in later years. There were, however, two variations from this standard pattern of naming style on the GWR which must be mentioned. Some of the earlier broad gauge engines, such as *North Star*, of which there is a replica in Swindon Museum, had individual brass letters attached to the framing, a feature also peculiar to the Bristol & Exeter Railway, although in this case it consisted of the company's initials and a number. Incidentally, it may be recalled that the famous single wheelers which worked much of the principal traffic until the abolition of the 7 ft gauge in 1892 were unique on a main line in that they were never given numbers. For a similar situation where the small stud of locomotives never carried numbers one must look to such modest concerns as the Isle of Wight, until the 1923 grouping, and in Ireland, the Sligo Leitrim & Northern Counties, right up to closure in 1957. The other variation in GWR practice lay in the original idea of using a large brass oval plate on the side of the cab which not only carried the number and name of the locomotive, but also information concerning the building details in lieu of a separate works plate. These were to be found only on some 4-4-0s of the *Bulldog* and *Atbara* classes built in 1899 and 1900.

The choice of GWR names covered an enormously wide range. Almost every conceivable subject has been used at some time or other, some repeated many times. The earlier engines were named after celebrated men, historical figures, geographical locations and heroes of myth and legend. A rather odder choice for an engine class was the 'Flowers' of GWR. This railway tended (in later years especially) to allocate specific themes to different classes of engines, which in consequence came to be collectively referred to as the 'Saints', 'Stars', 'Counties', 'Castles', 'Kings' and so on. The ultimate was achieved with the mixed traffic 'Hall' class introduced in 1928, of which the eventual total was no less than 330 engines. Somehow enough stately homes of England had been discovered by the time production ceased in 1950. The famous 'Kings' of 1927, named after the monarchs of England, starting with 6000 *King George V*, then on the throne, and working backwards, through the ages, got as far as *King Stephen* No 6029 before their construction ceased. Later, provision had to be made to accommodate *King Edward VIII* and *King George VI*.

With the coming of British Railways the Western Region still adhered to some GWR practices, and for a time continued its policy in the naming of express diesel locomotives. This was not followed to any extent by the other Regions and has now virtually been abandoned. The 'Warships' of 1958 nearly all perpetuated the practice of naming a class according to a particular theme, to be succeeded even more rigorously with the 'Westerns' in 1961, when all seventy-four engines became 'Western' something or other. The repetition of this magic word was no doubt balm to the large number of GWR devotees – *Western Champion* in particular might have seemed appropriate, although enough names were thought up without a *Western Enthusiast*. There was, however, a *Western Firebrand* which was perhaps even more suitable. Both of these classes had oblong nameplates on the side of the engine, the 'Warships' of definite GWR pattern with serif lettering, but degenerating into a plainer and much smaller type with the 'Westerns'. A few class 47s also perpetuated traditional Great Western names such as *North Star, City of Truro*, and *Isambard Kingdom Brunel*. Otherwise few BR diesels have received names, some in classes 40, 44, 45, 46 and all twenty-two Deltics, class 55. The seven main line electric locomotives for the Manchester–Sheffield scheme (now sold to the Dutch State Railway) were appropriately named, as were some of the mixed traffic engines of class 76. Official policy is now apparently against naming, a regrettable and backward step, for the soulless diesel or electric locomotive, lacking the glamour of steam, could well do with some distinction to give it a degree of interest.

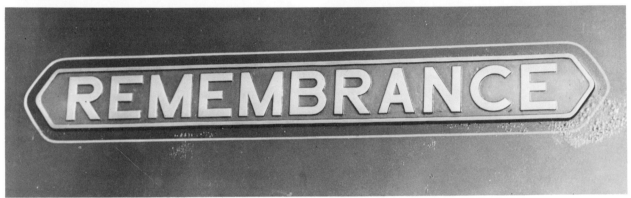

GWR combined name, number and works plate. Bulldog
class.
SR Repton. *Schools class.*
SR Remembrance. *Remembrance class.*
SR River Itchen. *River class.*

Reverting to pre-grouping days, apart from the LNWR and GWR, the railway most addicted to naming was the London Brighton & South Coast in Stroudley's time, but as the names were invariably painted on the engines and this account is chiefly concerned with nameplates, they come outside the scope of the review. Nearly all of Mr Stroudley's names were removed when D. Earle Marsh succeeded him. It is apposite, however, to mention at this point that the newly formed Southern Railway, shortly after the 1923 grouping embarked on an extensive publicity campaign which included a policy of naming its express engines, a practice which had long since been abandoned by its three principal constituents. Under this scheme the eleven Marsh Atlantics of the LBSCR received names of various promontories on the South Coast, such as *Beachy Head*, and these were displayed on two separate curved nameplates on each of the splashers over the driving wheels. The names of the Baltic tanks *Stephenson* and *Remembrance* were also perpetuated in the form of rectangular plates on the side tanks, but the few other engines which had managed to retain their names under the Marsh regime including the two fine 4-6-2Ts *Abergavenny* and *Bessborough* were not so honoured. Incidentally, when the seven Baltic tanks were later re-built as 4-6-0 tender engines, they were given names of former loco engineers of the SR constituents, in conformity with *Stephenson*, such as *Timothy Hackworth*. The war memorial engine *Remembrance*, also carried, in its rebuilt form, a suitable plaque in memory of LBSCR employees who had fallen during the 1914–18 war.

The only original SECR engine to be named was the prototype 2-6-4T No 790, which now became *River Avon*, to be followed by others newly built after the grouping and also named after rivers. These had nameplates on the tank sides. Of former LSWR engines, Urie's 736 class of 1918 was incorporated into Mr Maunsell's new 'King Arthurs' which appeared in 1925 and all of them were given names associated with the Knights of the Round Table, made in the form of rectangular plates on the very narrow elongated splasher. The subsequent 'Lord Nelson' and 'Schools' classes had similar plates, but of the curved type. After the grouping a number of Adams O2 class 0-4-4Ts were transferred to the Isle of Wight, where they were given names of local interest, displayed on oblong plates on the tank side. The background was painted red, which became general practice with other SR named engines of this period. Some LBSCR 0-6-0Ts of class A1X and E were also transferred to the island and named accordingly.

The last days of the Southern saw the appearance of Bulleid's Pacifics, the 'Merchant Navies' and the 'West Countries'. The 'Merchant Navies' carried appropriate names, such as *General Steam Navigation*, but in this case a combination type of plate was used incorporating the name of the shipping line and a reproduction of its house flag. The smaller Pacifics were given names of towns in the form of rectangular plates, often accompanied by a separate plate depicting the town's coat of arms. Later examples bore names commemorating the Battle of Britain, and are sometimes referred to as a separate class although there is no mechanical difference between the two series.

Some other companies of importance also named their locomotives, though none of these pursued the consistent policies of the LNWR or GWR. Several had somewhat spasmodic schemes, whereby they usually affixed names to the more important express engines. The Great Central, the development of the Manchester, Sheffield and Lincolnshire Railway, which had no named engines, introduced under J. G. Robinson a very limited policy of naming a few engines–this was developed to some extent over the years. Four of his D9 4-4-0s were selected in the first instance, together with all four compound Atlantics, but none of the much more numerous simple version. Some of Robinson's last designs of 4-4-0 and 4-6-0 however were named in their entirety. All of these had splasher nameplates, and one of them, No 1165 *Valour*, chosen as the 1914–18 War Memorial engine, also carried a suitably worded commemorative plate. The LBSCR *Remembrance* has already been referred to in this connection, but it may be mentioned here that a third railway to remember the casualties of the First World War was the LNWR, which exhibited a suitable plate on the splashers of one of its *Claughton* class 4-6-0s, the engine being named *Patriot*. In addition it was given the significant number 1914.

It may be recalled that Crewe had also given the special number 5000 to one of its 'George the Fifth' engines, to commemorate the five thousandth engine built there. As this happened to be the time of the coronation of George V, it was appropriately named *Coronation* and the plate was surmounted by a replica of the Imperial Crown, the Royal coat of arms being displayed on the splasher. Previously, in 1900, the 4000th engine *La France* had likewise been given the special number 4000, and again in 1950 the 7000th engine, Ivatt 2-6-2T No 41272 was provided with a suitable commemorative plaque on the tank sides.

The remaining major English railways of the pre-grouping era may be dealt with very briefly. As mentioned earlier, the Midland had but two named engines throughout its existence. The single wheeler *Princess of Wales* had its name hand painted on the splashers, but the 4-4-0 No 1757 *Beatrice* had a curved brass splasher plate. It was so named in honour of Princess Beatrice, who opened the Saltaire Exhibition in 1887 where the

One of SR's 'Merchant Navy's'.

engine was on view. Great Northern *Henry Oakley*, named after its then general manager, carried two separate brass plates on the twin splashers, and *Great Northern*, the first Gresley Pacific, which appeared just before the grouping, a curved plate, mounted above the very small splasher over the centre pair of driving wheels. Of the three Great Eastern engines, only *Claud Hamilton* boasted a brass plate somewhat similar to the LNWR style, but after re-building by Gresley in 1933 it was replaced by a standard LNER type. The other two, *Mogul* of 1878 (the first 2–6–0 in the British Isles) and oil fired 2–4–0 *Petrolea* of 1893, had painted names. The North Eastern quota included the well known *Aerolite*, preserved at York, and the first two of Raven's five Pacifics, which came out at the same time as the first two Gresley engines in the closing months of the pre-grouping era. The class, which totalled five engines, all received names of cities, but these were not applied until April 1924 and none appeared in NER livery. The Lancashire & Yorkshire abandoned a comprehensive naming policy very early on, and thereafter applied names only to its narrow gauge engines at Horwich works, which were unnumbered. These were names of birds (of which *Wren* has been preserved) and the small plates were mounted most unusually on the dome.

Passing now to the post grouping era, in 1927, with the appearance of the *Royal Scot* class, the recently formed London Midland and Scottish Railway inaugurated a general policy of naming all of its newly constructed express engines, which continued until nationalisation. The first batch of 'Scots' carried regimental names, but Nos 6125 and 6149 departed from this plan and for several years commemorated old locomotives. Moreover they added some most attractive oval brass plates on which were engraved etchings of the engines concerned. These included such famous and venerable names as *Sanspareil*, *Novelty*, *Lion*, *Jenny Lind*, and many others well known from this early period. Subsequent engines regrettably reverted to the regimental pattern. Few, if any, of these fascinating plaques depicting the old engines have survived. How eagerly they would have been sought after in these days, and what fantastic prices they would have commanded! Eventually the whole class of seventy engines acquired regimental appellations, if one can include No 6168 to 6169, *The Girl Guide* and *The Boy Scout*. The final rebuild No 6170, became *The British Legion*.

Other express types duly received names, the 'Patriots' a miscellaneous selection, but their successors, the 'Jubilees' bore many fine names associated with the British Empire, as it then was, together with admirals of the fleet, famous warships, and so on. The first Pacifics which came out in 1933–5, bore names of ladies of the Royal Family, mostly Princesses. After these came the 'Coronations', the absence of splashers necessitating a reversion to oblong plates mounted centrally on the side of the streamlined casing. This positioning was adopted even on non-streamlined engines.

The LNER also embarked on an extensive naming policy, starting with the Gresley Pacifics, of which many of the earlier examples received names of famous racehorses. Some of these seemed somewhat inappropriate when applied to a fine locomotive, such as *Sandwich* and *Spearmint*. They all had nameplates of the curved type over the splasher, as did the 'Shire' class 4–4–0s, and the 'Sandringham' 4–6–0s. The later 'Shires' were named after well known hunts, and the plates were surmounted by a replica of a fox. The earlier 'Sandringhams' were mostly connected with the stately homes of England, but the last batch took names of football teams and carried the respective club's colours.

The Gresley A4 Pacifics had the nameplate mounted forward on the streamlined casing, and his later engines, together with those of his successors, Thompson and Peppercorn, also had them placed well forward either on the side of the smokebox or on the smoke deflectors, where these existed, which provided a very convenient location in the absence of the old-time splashers. A few of the last LNER Pacifics, designed by A. H. Peppercorn, carried well chosen commemorative names associated with the constituents of the LNER, and five recalled some of the old companies, namely the Great Northern, North Eastern, Great Central, Great Eastern, and North British. These incorporated the old coats of arms of their respective railways, a happy inspiration.

It is not possible within the limited space available to go into detail of names applied to the smaller independent and light railways, still less to the numerous industrial engines under private ownership or the large collieries which eventually came under the National Coal Board, steelworks and the like, many of which were named at one time or another. Passing reference may be made to such lines as the Lynton & Barnstaple, Isle of Wight, and Plymouth Devonport & South Western Junction Railway, which were absorbed into the Southern, all of which carried nameplates on the tanksides, and one or two of the Welsh lines which went into the GWR. The two Leek & Manifold Light Railway locos which went into the LMS had the very rare combination of large oval plates embodying the name of the railway, number 1 and 2, and name, together with the builder's name and date of construction. The three major Welsh narrow gauge railways—Festiniog, Talyllyn, and Vale of Rheidol also named their locomotives as did the Isle of Man Railway and some of the Irish narrow gauge and minor lines.

LNWR Precedent class
BR(W) Warship class.
LMS Royal Scot class.
GNSR D40 class.

GWR Castle class.
LBSCR Atlantic H3 class.
LMS Jubilee class.
CIE Bia class.

A group of private works plates.

NER Aerolite.
LMS Meteor. *Royal Scot class.*
GNR(I) Meath. *U class.*

Mention should also be made of the Metropolitan Railway, which named its twenty electric locomotives used on the locomotive hauled trains out as far as Rickmansworth, beyond which they were steam hauled. These carried handsome plates in serif lettering with a decorative embellishment at either end. During World War II they were jettisoned in the 'save metal' campaign, but after the end of the war the names were reinstated with a new plate of a much plainer design. The Metropolitan also named its four 0–6–4T locomotives. Few electric locomotives have been honoured with names. The LNER ones have already been referred to, but there seems to be no intention of thus honouring the engines on Britain's premier main line, the West Coast route between London and Glasgow.

So far as steam locomotives are concerned, British Railways named its three classes of Pacifics, the 'Britannias', 'Clans' and the solitary *Duke of Gloucester*, these plates being placed on the smoke deflector at the side of the smokebox. A few 73000 Class 4–6–0s on the Southern Region were given names formerly carried by King Arthur class locomotives. These were rectangular and mounted above the central driving wheels, as there were no splashers to which they could be affixed. The last of the austerity 2–8–0s, built in such large numbers during the war, No 90732, was provided with a nameplate *Vulcan* (having been built by the Vulcan foundry) in an unusual position on the cabside. Two 2–10–0s, Nos 90773 and 90774, which came from the North British Loco Company carried identical names *North British* on the sides of the boiler. Then there was also No 92220 *Evening Star*, the last new BR steam engine: built at Swindon in 1960 it was graced by a splendid nameplate in true GWR style with serif lettering – the engine also carried a copper capped chimney.

For various reasons it was not uncommon for engines named to receive a permanent change, but this could sometimes be of a purely temporary nature for some special reason. For instance the LMS streamlined Pacific No 6229 *Duchess of Hamilton* went on tour to the USA disguised as No 6220 *Coronation*. Owing to the outbreak of war its return to this country was delayed for many months, but when it finally did get back it reverted to its old identity. Not so on a similar occasion, when 'Scot' No 6152 exchanged name and number with the original 6100 *Royal Scot*, and went on tour in America. In this case the changeover was permanent. SR 861 *Lord Anson* temporarily assumed the identity of No 850 *Lord Nelson* for the Liverpool Centenary celebrations in September 1930, whilst 'Schools' No 934 *St Lawrence* borrowed the nameplate of another of the class *Westminster* for working a special train on 21 March 1939 conveying the French President on a state visit to London. The funeral train of King George VI to Windsor was hauled by what pur-

ported to be an engine he had once driven on a visit to Swindon works and which was named *Windsor Castle*, but as this happened to be in the works at the time the number and nameplates were exchanged with No 7013 *Bristol Castle*, and in this case never altered back. Again, it was not unknown for such changes of identity to be effected temporarily for the purpose of taking an official photograph.

The Scottish lines must be dismissed somewhat perfunctorily, as they do not come strictly within the scope of this review. The Caledonian, North British, named a number of their engines, and the Highland in particular a large proportion of them, but all were hand painted and no plates were used. A few Great North of Scotland 4–4–0s, which came out in its last years, had the usual splasher type of nameplate, of which one, *Gordon Highlander*, can fortunately be seen in Glasgow Museum.

Going back somewhat in time and across the Irish Sea, three of the largest railways which adopted a general naming policy were the Great Northern the Midland Great Western and Dublin & South Eastern. Moreover at one period they differed from English companies in naming practically all of their engines, both passenger and goods: the latter usually had oblong plates on the boiler such as in earlier times. (The D&SER had painted names.) The GNR discontinued the practice about the time of World War I, and the names were removed: it was revived to a limited extent on the main passenger classes during the 1930s and 1940s. The MGWR and D&SER all lost their names at the Irish 1925 grouping when they became part of the Great Southern, which followed the former Great Southern and Western practice of only numbering engines. There were a few occasional exceptions, usually small tank locos, some of which as compensation, were unnumbered! The most important of these exceptions were the three large 4–6–0s, constructed in 1939, incidentally the last new steam engines to be built for the GSR, or CIE as it later became. These were endowed with names of former Irish Queens, *Maeve*, *Macha* and *Tailte*, displayed in Erse lettering in the usual position over the centre driving wheels.

Mr B. Malcolm, who built a number of two-cylinder Worsdell von Borries compounds for the Belfast & Northern Counties Railway, named a few of his 2–4–0s and 4–4–0s, but when the railway was taken over by the Midland in 1903 this was not continued. It was not until the line became part of the LMS after the grouping that a more general naming policy, applicable to the 4–4–0s, then the principal express type, was inaugurated, to be followed up with the 2–6–0s of Derby design, introduced in 1933. These had the usual curved plate over the splashers in the case of the 4–4–0s, and rectangular ones on the 2–6–0s, which had no splashers.

British Railways number plate (LM Region, following
LMS practice) with shed plate below indicating home
shed.

Turning now to the question of number plates, the numbering of engines was more important for distinguishing purposes where an increasingly large fleet was involved, and this began to be applied as a necessary procedure from the very early days. At first it was usually in the form of a cast metal plate, although on some railways it was not long before the much more economical method of painting the number was adopted. However, some lines continued with plates throughout their existence. LNWR number plates consisted of a rectangular brass plate, mounted on the cabside, tankside or bunker, bearing the number in handsome raised serif numerals, with a red background. In small lettering there was also the legend 'Crewe works', sometimes with the date of construction. The small LNWR offshoot in Ireland, the Dundalk Newry & Greenore Railway with its six 0–6–0STs, of unmistakeable Crewe design, had similar number plates, but with the appropriate substitution of the name of the railway. They also had nameplates to match on the side of the saddle tank. The Great Western adopted a standard number plate measuring 24in by 12in, very similar in size and shape, but in this case with a black background. They were usually of brass, but in later years cast iron was substituted for some of the less important classes. When the figures were kept polished, as they invariably were in pre-war days, they were easily

readable at a moderate distance, but latterly, when they became dirty, were difficult to decipher, especially in a bad light.

Occasionally individual brass figures were used, as on the Midland until 1907, and to most Wainwright engines built after the formation of the South Eastern & Chatham in 1900 right down to the grouping. Both constituents of this railway, the South Eastern and the London Chatham & Dover had used oval plates with the company's name around the edge. The SECR cast similar plates carrying the new title for these engines. During World War I the SECR changed its livery from green to black and adopted large painted numerals on the tender or tank side, Midland fashion. The number plates or brass figures disappeared, but their place was taken by a small rectangular plate bearing the initials SECR.

William Adams, whilst loco superintendent of the Great Eastern from 1873 to 1878, introduced a fairly large oval number plate with raised brass figures encircled by the company's name and the date of the engine's construction at Stratford works. The background was painted red. This remained standard until the end of the company's existence in 1923. Adams had meanwhile gone to the LSWR, where he introduced the same type of plate but without the building particulars, which this railway was always reluctant to display on its engines. His successor, Dugald Drummond, replaced

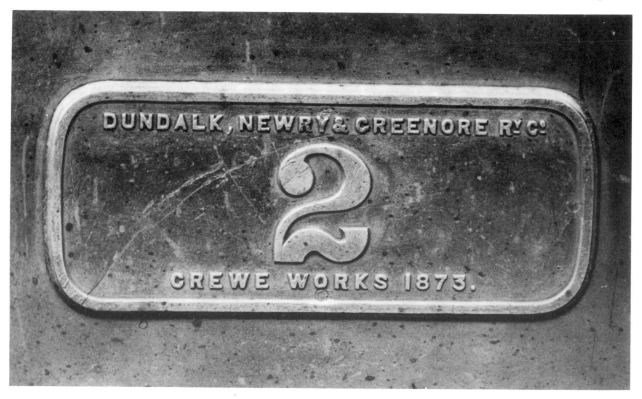

A Dundalk, Newry & Greenore Railway number plate.

A GER locomotive, built Stratford works, 1904.

Plate for a GWR locomotive, built Wolverhampton
works, 1896.

L&YR number plate for the first locomotive built at Horwich works.
Midland Railway painted numbers.
A Southern number plate of the mid-1920s. The prefix E stands for Eastleigh.

these with a brass plate with black recessed figures encircled by the words 'South Western Railway' similar to those he had used on the Caledonian, but these did not last long and were superseded by painted numerals.

William Stroudley, during his short term of office on the Highland between 1866 and 1869 built three engines (forerunners of his well known 'Terriers') with an oval plate carrying the company's name, which pattern he took to the LBSCR, where it remained standard until the end of the reign of his successor, R. J. Billinton in 1904. Earle Marsh, who followed him, however, had very different ideas: he introduced painted numerals, chocolate livery in place of Stroudley's yellow, and removed most of the names, which had always been of the painted variety.

Other larger railways which used varying types of number plate were the L&YR, NER, Cambrian, NBR and GNSR. The GNR from Stirling's time always used painted numerals. The Manchester, Sheffield & Lincolnshire also painted most of its numbers, but there were some few large oval plates encircled by the company's initials. Robinson on the reconstituted Great Central introduced plates with his single wheelers of 1900. The first of these were rectangular in shape, but soon gave way to the more usual oval pattern which lasted until the grouping. About the time the Midland introduced its comprehensive renumbering scheme in 1907 it also instituted the American practice of displaying the number in large painted figures on the tender or tank side. The individual brass figures disappeared, but these were still to be seen on the Somerset & Dorset Joint Railway, whose locomotive department was directed from Derby until 1930, when the stock was absorbed into the LMS, and likewise until 1937 on the Midland & Great Northern Joint Railway, when its engines were taken over by the LNER.

After the grouping both the LNER and the Southern in common with the LMS adopted large painted numerals on the tender or tank side, together with oval number plates on the cabside or bunker. Some SR tank engines had the plate on the back of the bunker or sometimes merely a painted number in this position. The SR number plate bore the words Southern Railway with the engine number below. This for the first few years included a letter prefix A (Ashford) for former SECR engines, B (Brighton) for LBSCR and E (Eastleigh) for LSWR. On the eventual renumbering of 1931 these had to be altered accordingly. From 1939 onwards the plates were removed and painted numerals substituted, the number no longer appearing in large format on the tank or tender sides. The LNER also included a standard type of number plate which embodied not only the company's name and engine number, but building particulars and year of construction. The removal of the brass figures on the Midland however was accompanied by the introduction of a number plate on the smokebox door. Most railways had a painted number plate on the front buffer beam, but some lines never had any front identification, not only the Midland itself up to this time, but also the LNWR and the L&YR throughout their existence, and the LBSCR in Stroudley's days.

The excellent and easily visible smokebox door plate was destined to become standard practice not only on the Midland, but in due course on the LMS at the grouping and eventually on BR at nationalisation. Crewe however had never taken kindly to Midland practices introduced after 1923 and so far as its own LNWR engines were concerned, fitted the new plates in a somewhat half hearted fashion and later actually removed most of them. In BR days it does not appear that any former LNWR locomotives ever received a new five-figure number plate. The Midland type of smokebox door plate was of cast iron with raised numerals of the handsome serif type, the figures usually being painted white for adequate visibility. This pattern continued to be used by the LMS until after the war, when it began to be replaced by a plainer pattern of figure. British Railways continued the practice, and nearly all of its engines (the LNWR excepted) were fitted, both new and those acquired from the other pre-nationalisation railways, the LNER, GWR and SR. The general standard adopted was the Gill Sans, although Derby continued to use the intermediate plain type (also Horwich to a certain extent), whilst some engines freshly renumbered (and even new ones built at Crewe in 1948) perpetuated the old serif pattern with their new five figure numbers, but these were later replaced by Gill Sans. Pending the renumbering scheme a few engines had an extension to the number plate to accommodate the regional prefix M, but it is not thought that any E or S engines appeared thus. GWR engine numbers, being in the four figure bracket were of course unchanged. The only BR diesel engines to receive number plates were the Western Region 'Hymeks' and 'Western' class: these were small oblong plates fitted to the cabside, the number being preceded by the letter D, diesel engines being at first so distinguished, as D7000. The electric engines for the West Coast main line had individual aluminium figures preceded by E, as E3001, but these were renumbered during 1973 and 1974, when the engines were renumbered in the 80000 series with painted numbers.

Shed Plates

At the same time as the Midland adopted smokebox door number plates back in 1907, it also introduced the practice of indicating the engine's home shed by means

Great Central 'Atlantic' locomotive with coat of arms, monogram, name and number plate all visible.

of a small circular plate lower down on the smokebox, bearing the shed's individual code number, which ranged from 1 (Derby) to 33 (Carlisle). Few other railways adopted this practice, although the LNWR and the L&YR displayed a similar sort of plate on the back of the cab roof, also carrying the respective code number. The LBSCR indicated the shed by a lettered code, such as T-WELLS, at the front end of the framing, and the GWR did the same with such codes as RDG

indicating Reading, or TYS for Tyseley. The SECR carried the numbered shed code inside the cab on the right hand panel.

The Midland type of shed plate on the smokebox door was adopted as standard by British Railways, a new shed code being drawn up to embrace all regions. This entailed, in addition to the number which indicated the main depot, a letter suffix in respect of the various sub sheds. These numbers ranged from 1 to 27 allocated to the LM regions, 30 to 41 for the Eastern, the North Eastern in the 50s, Scottish the 60s, Southern the 70s and Western the 80s. The cast iron plates were 7in wide

and 5in in height. BR diesels and electric locomotives have not normally carried any shed identification, although a painted replica of the shed plate appeared on a few diesels on the Eastern region, as for instance 34G indicating Finsbury Park.

Works Plates

The remaining form of adornment of the kind under review is the works plate of the maker. Some railways, notably the LNWR, GWR, GNR, GER, NER, LSWR, SECR, LBSCR and others built most of their engines in their own workshops, at Crewe, Swindon, Doncaster, Darlington or Gateshead etc, but others, especially the smaller ones had recourse to the outside private firms, of which there were many. These firms also built large numbers of locomotives for export to all parts of the world, and not unnaturally took the opportunity of advertising themselves with a plate mounted on the engine bearing their name and location. The plates also carried the works number of the locomotive for easy reference back to the factory when overhauls or spare parts, even drawings were required.

Some railways also provided such information in respect of engines built in their own workshops, often

A group of railway company works plates.

embodied on the number plate itself. The LNWR and GER have already been mentioned in this respect. The GNR, GCR, HR and LBSCR were among the lines which provided individual building plates. The GNR produced two kinds, a cast iron one with raised lettering, and also a larger brass type with recessed figures and words, including not only the year of construction but also the Doncaster works number. This was unusual, for railway companies did not often incorporate such information as the private builders did. The South Eastern & Chatham employed a standard brass oval plate inscribed 'Constructed at Ashford works, SE&CR' but without any other details Midland engines carried a small oval plate which carried the inscription 'Midland Railway, built Derby' followed by the year of construction, or 'rebuilt' with the appropriate date. At one period it was the practice to use the wording 'boiler new' with the date, this apparently being regarded as of supreme importance. This type of plate was continued upon the formation of the London Midland & Scottish Railway and used by the works of the other absorbed railways, but it was backdated on pregrouping engines, new plates being

cast with absurd titles such as 'LMS built Inverness 1900', many years before such a concern had been remotely dreamed of. The LNER carried out a similar operation, in this case it took the form of a combined number and works plate, and has already been mentioned. For some reason both railways seemed anxious in these early years to eradicate the memory of the former companies. The Southern did not embody any form of separate ownership on building works plates.

Private builders' plates took various forms, some of the earlier ones were quite ornate in appearance, but these gradually settled down to a circular, oblong, rectangular or diamond shaped plate of brass or cast iron, giving the name of the makers, the town at which their works were situated, the year of construction, and usually but not always, the works number. The first firm of private builders was formed in 1823 by George Stephenson himself in conjunction with his son Robert, in whose name the company was founded. In later years it was amalgamated with another firm, Hawthorn Leslie & Co, and the new firm took the name of Robert Stephenson & Hawthorns Ltd. As such it was building engines to the end of the steam age, a direct link with the father of the steam locomotives. Many other firms were established over the years, some short-lived but many continuing production right to the end. Among such famous builders were Manning Wardle, Beyer Peacock & Co, Kitson & Co, Hunslet Engine Co, Hudswell Clarke, Vulcan Foundry, Yorkshire Engine Co, Peckett & Sons, Sharp Stewart, Neilson, and Dübs & Co, the last three of which eventually amalgamated to form the North British Locomotive Company, and many others. Specimens of the works plates of most of these firms can be found not only on preserved locomotives but separately in museums and in numerous private collections all over the country.

So far as nameplates are concerned, it was possible before the war to obtain from some of the railway companies' (the GWR and LMS in particular) plates from withdrawn engines at practically the scrap value of the brass. Now the value of such trophies has risen to astronomical heights. Such has become the craze in recent years for acquiring relics from steam locomotives in this handy form that nameplates, number plates, and even such minor items as shed plates are eagerly sought after. The regrettable story of how many of these items have been acquired other than by legitimate means over the last decade is well enough known, and not to the credit of enthusiasts in general. In the later years of steam, engines at sheds could be found to have mysteriously 'lost' their plates overnight, and even those still lovingly preserved by voluntary organisations have to be well protected against vandalism. Of the two hundred or so engines which have been standing at Barry scrapyard during the last few years, not one retains the vestige of a name or number plate, or even any other easily removable fitting. It is only fair to add that many of these were removed by genuine prospective buyers of the engine for obvious security reasons. However, it is pleasant to be able to record that so many reminders of the great steam age still remain in existence, whether in private hands or on exhibition in museums.

This works plate is a wartime oddity. It was made for a Stanier LMS 2-8-0 built in Southern Railway workshops for the LNER. Beneath it are two locomotive shed plates belonging respectively to the London Midland and Western Region of BR. C. M. Whitehouse Collection.

A group of private works plates.

Clocks and Watches

E. J. Tyler

The importance of accurate timekeeping had been recognised in the days of the stage coaches. Inns where coaches stopped were provided with wall clocks having large legible dials and the guards of mail coaches were supplied with special watches in rectangular brass cases to check the running of the coach. Stops to change horses were frequent, and in a journey like London to Manchester, three minutes' delay at each of twenty stops would make the coach one hour late.

When the railways began to develop, the speed was much greater than that of the coaches, and as they worked on a time interval system, accurate timekeeping was more important than ever. Stations were provided with clocks as the inns had been, but the issuing of watches to the staff appears to have been limited at first.

The higher speed emphasised a difficulty that had existed in the coaching days, namely that every place in the country kept its local time. A passenger whose watch was recording the correct time at Paddington would arrive at Bristol to find the station clocks apparently ten minutes slow, and if he relied on station clocks at each end to time his journey, he would apparently have taken ten minutes less than was actually the case. The LNWR brought matters to a head in 1847 by standardising Greenwich time over their system and other lines followed suit. A proposal was made in 1852 to telegraph the time to signal boxes every day and this idea was brought into use later, giving a special sanctity to railway time and causing people to visit the station to set their watches.

In the early days of the London and Southampton Railway, the drivers had no watches, but were timed by station staffs and told if the preceding trains were late. After 1840 station clocks were given two dials so that train crews could see the time and the station clocks were regulated by the guard of the first train down every day. In December 1841 a Mr Walker undertook to maintain all clocks on the system for £20 per annum.

The principal railway stations were provided with turret clocks not only to record the time but also as a status symbol. At the Great Exhibition of 1851 Dents exhibited a turret clock which was purchased by the GNR for their new terminus at Kings Cross. Although this clock struck, the striking has been silent for many years. Just across the way, the Midland terminus of St Pancras has its clock tower, and other examples of large clocks on railway stations are those at Liverpool Street and Bristol Temple Meads.

Not only have the turret clocks on stations become well known, but also those on the companies' workshops and depots such as Nine Elms, Ashford, New Cross Gate and Crewe. Many of these have disappeared long since, and are known only from photographs.

These large clocks can scarcely be considered collectors' items, and it is therefore the smaller clocks on the station platforms that are more likely to be of interest. Most of the railway clocks were of the type known to the Trade as the 'English Dial', which was also extensively used in offices, shops, etc. In these clocks the dial proper is usually about 12 inches in dia-

Weight driven platform clock, c. 1890, as used on the LSWR and LBSCR.

meter although larger and smaller sizes have been made. Sometimes the case is extended below it to allow a longer pendulum which makes for greater accuracy. The movement has solid brass plates and the varying tension of the mainspring as it runs down is compensated for by a device known as a fusee, which resembles a truncated cone and has a gut line or a chain wrapped round it which gradually winds off as the clock runs down. This type of clock began to be made about 1780, but was not used to a large extent for timing coaches, which were mostly regulated by the weight driven clocks previously mentioned. Later modified versions of these weight driven clocks have also been used extensively on railway stations, and examples have been noted in recent years at Bramber (Brighton to Horsham line, now closed) and New Malden, LSWR. As these clocks were weight driven, they did not need a fusee, and the longer pendulum provided an even greater standard of accuracy.

Occasionally one meets a clock that is a little more elaborate than usual, and probably that in the shareholders' room at Euston was the best known. There is, or was, a fine specimen on the up platform at Gravesend.

The firm of Thwaites and Reed, which is still in existence, was supplying clocks to railways from 1837 onwards. Among other lines they supplied the London and Birmingham, London and Croydon, Birmingham and Derby Junction and North Midland. The usual price for a 12in dial in a mahogany case was £6 at this period, and a chain to the fusee was specified in place of a gut line as it was stronger. Many clocks were fitted with an 'Up and Down' indicator to show when they needed winding. All work would have been of the best English quality.

Certain railways had regulators supplied by the firm and these were fitted with 12 leaf pinions to improve the gearing and give a more even torque through the train, and some of the pivot holes and the pallets were also jewelled. These clocks would be the standard for regulating all the other clocks on the system.

The suppliers often did cleaning and repairs in the early days, but the railways soon established their own workshops for this. W. R. Sykes, the signal engineer, formerly worked in the clock repairs department of the LC&DR before specialising on signals. A description of the GWR repair shop appeared in the GWR staff magazine about thirty-five years ago.

Opposite page:
French clock in marble, for office use, c. 1880. Similar clocks were to be found in many homes throughout Britain.
Right:
GWR weight driven platform clock, c. 1870.

Highland Railway 'regulator', c. 1880, a clock which gives a very high standard of accuracy for controlling other clocks and watches. M. V. E. Dunn Collection.

London & Birmingham Railway 'regulator' clock, 1838, formerly at Euston Station.

Turret clock, formerly at Barking, LTSR. The movement can be seen in the central portion of the case. National Railway Museum.

While many lines relied on English suppliers for their station clocks, this was not a universal practice. The Caledonian made use of clocks by the firm of Winterhalder and Hofmeyer in Neustadt, Black Forest, who made clocks of the English type using high quality materials, but charged a very much lower price. Their movements are often indistinguishable from English ones in appearance but the little monogram on the back plate, 'W & H SCH' gives them away. The GNR on the other hand relied on Stockall Marples of Clerkenwell, a firm that ceased operation in 1970, while the LSWR got their clocks from John Walker.

The now popular electric clocks had their predecessors earlier in the century. The new Waterloo station of 1922 had the famous four dial clock in the centre of the circulating area and another dial over the exit by Platform 21. The London Underground fitted clocks by the Self Winding Clock Co and occasionally one could hear the electrical mechanism function as the clock was wound automatically. There was one at Aldwych a few years ago. Replacement of clocks is taking place on such a large scale that there is little purpose in stating that any type of timekeeper can be found at a certain place. Before these words are in print, it may well have disappeared.

A further burst of activity in railway clock supplies occurred just after nationalisation. It was found that about two hundred licensed refreshment rooms were breaking the law by not having a clock, and clocks were immediately ordered from a Clerkenwell firm and supplied to all regions in the neighbourhood of London. They were probably the last spring driven clocks ordered by the railways before the fashion for electric clocks came in.

The companies' offices also needed clocks and while many of the English Dial type were in use, ordinary domestic clocks are also seen bearing the companies' initials, in wooden, marble or metal cases. In the very early days, wall clocks with exposed weights and pendulums from the Black Forest were used, but their mortality rate was high and few, if any, have survived. The LNER magazine in 1945 carried an illustration of one of these clocks marked 'Monkland Railways', dating from the first half of the 19th century, and the writer saw one in use at March (Cambs.) station about thirty years ago.

The field for collectors of railway watches is much wider than that of clocks. Not only were there many more of them in use, but the companies seem to have cast their net wider in purchasing them. The information on this subject is by no means complete, as new specimens examined usually add to the list of suppliers. The earliest were of the English fullplate lever type and also incorporated a fusee, but later examples were

Above:
GWR portable clock by Kay of Paris, late 19th century. This type of clock was well known in domestic use, but railway examples are rare. John Adams Collection.

Opposite page:
Caledonian Railway 'English Dial' with long pendulum, c. 1890. Although indistinguishable from an English made example, the clock was actually produced by Winterhalder and Hofmeyer in Germany.

English three-quarter plate without fusees and Swiss and American watches were also used.

Among the oldest still to be seen are some in the Transport Museum at Glasgow. They were supplied by John Walker, Princes Street, Soho, and one of them was worn by the guard of the train that was wrecked in the Tay Bridge disaster of 1879. They bear the initials of the Edinburgh and Glasgow Railway, which means that they were made before 1865 as this line was amalgamated with the North British in that year.

E&GR No 25 is like the guard's watch of a mailcoach and bears the name 'Thornton, Paris', while NBR guards watch No 1 is by J. W. Benson, Ludgate Hill, London.

The Caledonian and Glasgow and South Western Railways used extra large English fullplate keywind watches with fusees at first, but later used the Swiss make 'Peerless'.

The South Eastern Railway had a batch of watches from Benson of Ludgate Hill which were stem wind

Above:
Clock in the Great Hall at Euston, as altered by the makers in 1849. Now National Railway Museum.

Opposite page:
Clock at Snow Hill Station, Birmingham, c. 1911.

three-quarter plate, but although the parts were standardised throughout most of the movement, the escapements were all individually fitted and the parts were not interchangeable. These watches come as a surprise, for older SER watches by Waltham, USA have been seen with all parts interchangeable although they were key wound. It was the practice of American factories to supply the movements only and the purchasers would arrange to have them put in cases. An example of this is a Seth Thomas movement in a case by A. L. Dennison of Birmingham for the S&DJR. This watch is a key wind but has no seconds hand. Later practice favoured seconds hands on rail-

way watches but it was not universal in the early days. This particular watch was made about 1890.

The LBSCR also used Waltham watches and had their initials on the dial which would have involved a special arrangement with the factory and also the ordering of a large number at a time.

A GWR watch has been seen with the name of Kays of Worcester on the dial. This is a well known firm but does not produce watches itself, hence any sold with this name must have been obtained from other suppliers while the vendor's name acts as a guarantee. This practice has been known in the horological trade for at least two centuries.

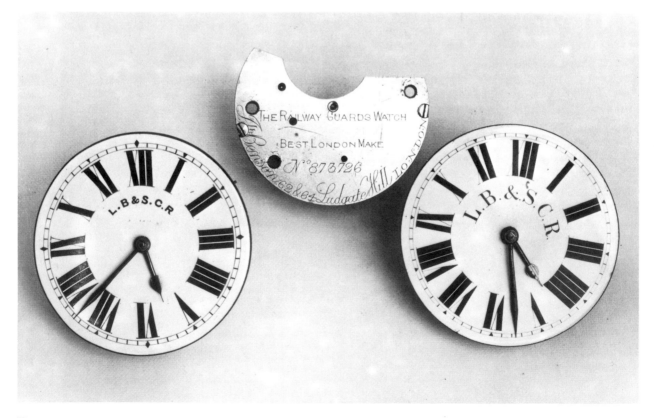

Top:
Two very early railway watches. The one on the right was supplied by John Walker for the Edinburgh and Glasgow Railway. Transport Museum, Glasgow.

Above:
Two railway watch movements of the LBSCR supplied by Waltham, USA. The back plate comes from an SER watch and is London made.

Three railway watches. Top: a Waltham for the South Eastern Railway, centre: a watch for the same line made by J. W. Benson, London, below: watch by Seth, Thomas, Connecticut for the Somerset & Dorset Joint.

GWR watch, c. 1920. The projection on the case above the figure 1 is a stud for setting the hands. P. B. Whitehouse Collection.

LNER watch by Selex, c. 1930. The winding button is bigger than on earlier examples. P. B. Whitehouse Collection.

The LSWR marked their watches 'Goods' and 'Passenger' but there does not seem to be any reason for this. All trains used the same tracks and an equally accurate watch is needed for running goods as for passenger trains. The LSWR used the Swiss brand 'Cyma' among others, while the GNR(I) used 'Omega'.

Mention should also be made of the unofficial watches. A watch shown to the writer some years ago was supplied by Graves of Sheffield who ran an extensive mail order business about the turn of the century. Graves' watches often had 'The Express English Lever' marked on the dial. This particular watch was used by an LBSCR goods guard for many years although not company's issue. Graves usually got his supplies from the Lancashire Watch Co of Prescot, which existed 1889–1910. The company was founded to combat foreign competition by adopting American factory methods, but it came too late. The excessive conservatism in the trade led to such things as the SER Benson watches previously mentioned where individual fitting took place, and the cost of the product as a result of this helped to drive it off the market.

In their catalogue of 1905 the Lancashire Watch Co advertise a model called the 'Vigilant' as being popular with railways and describe it as a full plate, keyless,

fully jewelled and adjusted for variations of temperature and position. In nickel cases 'as supplied to railway companies £3–3–0. Non magnetic 10/- extra'. An example of this model with LNWR on the dial has been noted.

The firm of J. N. Masters of Rye, Sussex advertising on the rear cover of 'Locomotives and Railways' which began publication in January 1900, offers 'a silver cased keywind watch for 30/- with a free real silver albert in lieu of discount for cash. Railwaymen are invited to pay 5/- per month for this watch. No references or security required and no formalities. Send name and address with first payment of 5/- stating occupation and station engaged at, when watch is forwarded by return.' The watch is described as the most perfectly constructed watch ever offered to the public, but as it only possesses a horizontal escapement (not a lever) it would not be accurate enough for railway use although probably many railway staff would have worn them.

Many of the cheaper Swiss watches also bore the inscription 'Railway Timekeeper' or similar wording, but they are not to be compared with the watches actually used by the companies for issue to the staff, which were made to much more exacting requirements.

LNWR watch, c. 1900, made by the Lancashire Watch Company, Prescot. P. B. Whitehouse Collection.

Bibliography

D'Agapeyeff, A. and Hadfield, E. C. R. *Maps*. Oxford University Press. 1942

Biddle, G. and Fells, P. *Victorian Stations: Railway Stations in England and Wales 1836–1923*. David & Charles. 1973

Burridge, F. H. A. *Nameplates of the LMS*. Ian Allan. 1947

Burridge, F. H. A. *Nameplates of the LNER*. Ian Allan. 1947

Burridge, F. H. A. *Nameplates of the GWR*. Ian Allan. 1947

Burridge, F. H. A. *Nameplates of the SR*. Ian Allan. 1947

Byles, C. B. *First Principles of Railway Signalling*. Railway Gazette. 1910

Casserley, H. C. *British Locomotive Names: 20th Century*. Ian Allan. 1963

Casserley, H. C. *Locomotives at Grouping* (4 vols: *LMS, LNER, GWR, SR*). Ian Allan. 1966

Christiansen, Rex *A Regional History of the Railways of Great Britain: West Midlands*. David & Charles. 1974

Close, Colonel Sir Charles *The Early Years of the Ordnance Survey*. First published 1926. Reprinted David & Charles. 1969

Davis, W. J. and Waters, A. W. *Tickets and Passes of Great Britain*. Leamington Spa Publications. 1922

Disney, Henry W. *The Law of Carriage by Railway*. Stevens & Sons 1905. 7th edition 1928

Dow, George *Railway Heraldry*. David & Charles. 1973

Gardiner, R. S. *History of the Railway Ticket*. First published 1898. Reprinted for private circulation, Boston, Mass., 1938

Haskell, Daniel C. *A Tentative Check-List of Early Railway Literature 1831–1848*. Harvard School of Business Administration, Boston, Mass. 1955

Kitchenside, G. M. and Williams, A. *British Railways Signalling*. First published 1963. Reprinted Ian Allan. 1975

Lee, Charles E. *The Centenary of 'Bradshaw'*. The Railway Gazette. 1940

McDermot, E. T. *History of the Great Western Railway*. First published 1927. Reprinted Ian Allan, 1964

Royde Smith, G. *The History of 'Bradshaw'*. Henry Blacklock & Co. 1939

Tweedie, M. G. and Lascelles, T. S. *Modern Railway Signalling*. Gresham Publishing Co. About 1930

Vaughan, A. *Great Western Signalling*. Oxford Publications. 1973

Wiener, Prof. Lionel *Passenger Tickets*. The Railway Gazette. 1939

Williams, C. *Locomotives of the LNWR*. Privately printed in several editions before 1921

Wilson, R. B. *Go Great Western: A History of GWR Publicity*. David & Charles. 1970

Locomotives of the GWR (12 parts to 1974). Railway Correspondence and Travel Society

Locomotives of the LNER (Part 1). Railway Correspondence & Travel Society. 1974

Modern Railway Administration (2 vols). Gresham Publishing Co. 1927

Railway Signalling and Communications. St Margaret's Technical Press. 1940

Photographic Acknowledgements

Photographs were kindly provided by the following:
Black and White: Adams, John: 10, 11 *(below)*, 14, 15, 21, 24, 25, 26, 27, 28 *(both subjects)*, 29, 30, 32 *(above)*, 34, 48 *(left)*, 87 *(left)*, 114, 117, 121, 155, 160, 161, 162 *(left)*, 164, 165, 170 *(both subjects)*, 171; Alexander, P. M: 137 *(bottom)*, 139 *(top left)*, 149 *(below)*; Biddle, Gordon: 46 *(top row left, top row right, bottom row left, bottom row centre, bottom row right)*, 50 *(left and right)*, 52 *(bottom)*; Birmingham Post & Mail: 167; Bodleian Library, Oxford: 38; Bray, Maurice: 20 *(both subjects)*, 23 *(both subjects)*, 31, 32 *(below)*, 39; British Rail: 13, 16, 22, 43, 48 *(right)*, 49, 79, 81, 99, 100, 101, 102, 111, 115, 118, 119 *(both subjects)*, 120, 124 *(below)*, 128 *(below)*, 129, 131, 141, 150 *(top)*, 156 *(centre)*, 162 *(right)*, 163, 166; Casserley, H. C: 58 *(below left)*, 137 *(centre)*, 139 *(centre and bottom)*, 145 *(top and centre)*, 148, 149 *(above)*, 150 *(centre and bottom)*, 152, 154 *(all four subjects)*, 156 *(top and bottom)*, 157 *(above)*; Dow, Andrew: 128 *(above left and right)*; Dow, George: 124 *(above)*, 133, 135; Michael Dyer Associates: 67, 68, 69, 74, 77, 91, 92, 93, 94, 95, 96, 97, 110, 112, 113 *(both subjects)*, 116 *(above)*, 122; Gammell, C. J: 159; Gell, F. B: 57, 60 *(both subjects)*, 61 *(both subjects)*, 62 *(above)*, 63, 64 *(above)*, 65 *(above)*, 82, 83, 84, 86, 87 *(right)*; Gurley, N. F: 80 *(top left)*; Hinchley, B: 12; Read, R. E. G: 45, 46 *(top row centre)*, 51, 52 *(top and centre)*; Spence, Jeoffry: 40, 42; Thomas, Graham: 58 *(top left)*, 62 *(below)*, 64 *(below)*, 65 *(below)*; Thomas, Howard: 147; Whitehouse, C. M: 11 *(above)*, 80 *(below left)*; Whitehouse, P. B: 9, 58 *(right)*; 59, 80 *(right)*, 85 *(above)*, 132, 137 *(top)*, 139 *(top right)*, 145 *(bottom)*, 157 *(below)*.

Colour: Adams, John: 17 *(below)*, 18, 35, 36 *(below)*, 53 *(below)*, 72 *(below)*, 108 *(above)*, 144 *(top row left and right)*, 144 *(second row right)*, 144 *(third row right)*; British Rail: 71; Dow, George: 125 *(all three subjects)*, 126 *(top row left and centre)*, 126 *(second row centre and right)*, 126 *(third row left)*; Michael Dyer Associates: 36 *(above)*, 72 *(above)*, 89, 90; New English Library: 108 *(below)*; Semmens, P. W. B: 54; Whitehouse C. M: 17 *(above)*, 144 *(second row left)*, 144 *(third row left)*, 144 *(fourth row right)*; Whitehouse, P. B: 53 *(above)*, 126 *(top row right)*, 126 *(second row left)*, 126 *(third row centre and right)*, 126 *(bottom row, all three subjects)*, 143 *(all eight subjects)*, 144 *(fourth row left)*.

The endpapers illustrate part of the M. V. E. Dunn collection of railway relics. Photograph by the owner.